The Red Umbrella

Danish Resistance & Johna's Escape from Nazi Occupation

by
Johna Christensen

The Red Umbrella

Christensen, Johna

ISBN: 978-0-692-01661-9

Library of Congress Control Number: 2012936562

Printed in the United States of America

Christensen Publishing Company
P.O. Box 5068, Bellingham, WA 98227
www.red-umbrella.com

Contents

Prologue

The complexity of being such a young narrator and recalling my memories became crystal clear, as I struggled to put my frightened time in Nazi-occupied Denmark down on paper,

My living family assured me, to their amazement, that my memories of this time in my life, were very accurate. I had retained much about the harsh realities of war that had dismantled my safe, secure world. It had a profound effect upon the rest of my life for feeling safe.

These remembrances have compelled me to write my story, especially for my brother David Christensen and my sister Linda Christensen, that were born after the war in the United States of America.

- Johna Christensen

Foreword

Johna Christensen unexpectedly passed away on December 29, 2002, prior to this publication. As her brother, I was 16 years younger, and the first one of the Christensen family born in America after the War. I never learned much about the War years from our parents, because it was not something to discuss anymore. There was prejudice for new European immigrants to the United States and our parents wanted to fit in, including not speaking Danish often. (Except when they didn't want me to know what they were saying). I learned about this story of *The Red Umbrella* mostly from my visits with Johna, as she left home when she was 18. Our parents passed away when I was only 11 years old, so I was never able to get the whole story from them. As Johna got older, she had a strong desire to reconnect with our family in Denmark and to tell her story during World War II. I read drafts of the manuscript as Johna tried to find a publisher. Since her passing, her children (Charles, Clint and Jette) as well as my younger sister Linda and I, started the process to get this in print.

The Red Umbrella is a brief memoir of Johna's childhood and family life during the Nazi occupation of Denmark, told from her perspective as a six to eight year old from 1943-1945.

We had an Orthodox Jewish mother and a Danish father, who was not religious at all. So, the story played out against conflicting family and religious issues. In addition to the complications of the Nazi Occupation, Johna was Jewish and born without a Left hand, due to a birth defect. The Nazi occupation added a dimension of danger to the situation, that imperiled our parents during the Gestapo hunt for Danish Jews. At the same time, our father, Poul, was active in a growing Danish resistance movement.

Our Mother and her Jewish Parents hid, while Johna stayed behind with our Father. His dangerous activities included befriending some Nazi's at our Danish Grandmother's tavern and brothel.

From beginning to end, Johna's story is very touching

and dramatic, especially as written from a child's point of view. It is a desperate time, where women and men of courage and character are forced to be both heroes and villains.

Some readers may be unfamiliar with the amazing Danish Resistance of Nazi Occupation of Denmark in World War II. To give some context to this personal memoir, it may be important to know the circumstances going on outside of Johna's immediate world.

It was on October 1st 1943, when Hitler ordered Danish Jews to be arrested and deported. However, on September 28, 1943, word was leaked of the plans for this operation. The Jews were promptly warned of the German action and urged to go into hiding immediately and to spread the word to all their Jewish friends and relatives. Some simply phoned friends and asked them to go through telephone books and warn those with Jewish-sounding names to go into hiding. Most Jews hid for several days or weeks, uncertain of their fate.

The early phases of the rescue were improvisational. Although the majority of the Danish Jews were in hiding, they would eventually have been caught if safe passage to Sweden could not be secured.

The Jews were smuggled out of Denmark over the Øresund strait to Sweden—a passage of varying time depending on the specific route and the weather, but averaging under an hour on the choppy winter sea. Some were transported in large fishing boats of up to 20 tons, but others were carried to freedom in rowboats or kayaks. Some of the fishermen assisting in the rescue charged money to transport Jews to Sweden, while others took payments only from those who could afford passage. The Danish underground took an active role in organizing the rescue and providing financing, mostly from wealthy Danes who donated large sums of money to the endeavor.

During the first days of the rescue action, Jews moved into the many fishing harbors on the Danish coast for rescue, but the Gestapo became suspicious of activity around harbors. Subsequent rescues had to take place from isolated points along the coast. While waiting their turn, the Jews took refuge away from the coast, out of sight of the Gestapo. Danish harbor police and civil police often cooperated with the rescue effort.

The casualties among Danish Jews during the Holocaust were among the lowest of all occupied countries in Europe.

Although the Danish authorities initially cooperated with the German occupation forces, most Danes strongly opposed the isolation of any group within the population, especially the well-integrated Jewish community. The German action to deport Danish Jews prompted the Danish state church and political parties to denounce the action and to pledge solidarity with the Jewish fellow citizens. For the first time, they openly opposed the occupation.

The unsuccessful German deportation attempt and the actions to save the Jews were important steps in linking the resistance movement to broader anti-Nazi sentiments in Denmark. In many ways October 1943 and the rescuing of the Jews marked a change in most people's perception of the war and the occupations.

Despite great personal risk, the Danish resistance movement, with the assistance of many ordinary Danish citizens, took part in a collective effort to evacuate about 8,000 Jews of Denmark by sea to nearby neutral Sweden.

The rescue allowed the vast majority of Denmark's Jewish population to avoid capture by the Nazis and is considered to be one of the largest actions of collective resistance to repression in the countries occupied by Nazi Germany. As a result of the rescue and Danish Intercession on behalf of the Jews, over 99% of Denmark's Jewish population survived the Holocaust.

Johna's personal story during this time, adds her personal experiences for both our Danish family, and the Danish Jews. It is a very touching, and true story, so that we never forget. Johna lived her life as the eternal optimist, always ready for a good time with family and friends. As she always said, "...every day was a gift."

- David Earl Christensen

Dedication

This story is dedicated to the memory of my loving mother, Jette Malka Pressmann Christensen; my father, Poul Villy Christensen; my beloved Jewish grandparents, Yechiel Jacob Pressmann and Brochr Miriam Pressmann; my Jewish uncle, Willy Pressmann, his wife, my Aunt Marie, and my cousin Chaja Faltved, who also escaped Nazi-occupied Denmark, and to their daughter, Ruth, who stayed behind in Copenhagen, hidden by a Danish family; and to my Danish uncle, Arne Dam Hansen, who helped my father in the resistance.

Lastly, I dedicate this book to a dear family friend, Martin Travis, a survivor of Auschwitz.

- Johna Christensen

Chapter 1

The Dainty Swastika

My story begins one rainy day in early August, 1943, a time when much of the world was at war. My best friend Hanne Hansen and I were walking home from school, sharing Hanne's beautiful red umbrella. We were six years old then, and in the second grade together.

Only a few weeks and little else separated Hanne and me. While she was long-boned, blond, and blue-eyed, I had black curly hair and a darker complexion. We were both Danish, but she was not Jewish, like me. I also wore little round black-framed glasses, was shorter than she was, and my left arm ended in a point with five tiny stubs on it half way down my forearm. These differences meant nothing then, though we would come to know their importance in the days to come.

We were on our way to the neighborhood grocery store in Valby, the small town where we lived that was part of Copenhagen, Denmark. We thought the storekeepers there looked like movie actors we enjoyed. One was tall and thin like Stanley Laurel, and the other was short and round like Oliver Hardy. We had hopes they might give us candy. We knew they would certainly make us laugh.

"I can make a bigger splash than you," said Hanne, as she ran ahead of me to the next big puddle.

"Wait for me!" I cried, and ran around the puddle, not wanting to wet my shoes.

"Look out!" said Hanne, and she jumped into the puddle with both feet, splashing water up onto our coats. We hugged each other and laughed. It was that easy to have fun.

We soon continued on our way, eager to get to the store. We often stopped there after school. Big crates of fruit and vegetables always flowed out across the sidewalks in front of the store, and a pickle barrel sat near the entrance where the tart smell grabbed your nose as you passed by. At Christmas time, they would have big boxes of beautiful, round oranges, but it was too early for them that time of year. Inside the store, glass jars and open boxes of candy lined the counter. I would put my hand in the jars, as if I were taking some candy, and then 'Hardy' would see me and make a big show of running me off. It was a great game we played, for he often gave me candy in the end.

We had almost reached the store when suddenly we heard the thunderous noise of planes over our heads and the roar of tanks echoed off the surrounding buildings. When we turned the corner, we saw the planes, more than I could count, as they swarmed under the low rain clouds like dragonflies, each one dropping hundreds of papers with pictures of Hitler on them.

Denmark was Nazi-occupied territory then, and had been since April of 1940. The occupation had been a peaceful one, with things going along on the surface of life pretty much as they had before. Some Danes even welcomed the Germans, feeling some sympathy with the Nazi Party's emphasis on strength and purity. People had heard things about Jews being rounded up in Germany and other countries and put in concentration camps, even killed, but it was not certain knowledge, and nothing we children knew anything about. The worst of that was not to be known until after the war was over.

All Hanne and I knew was the Germans had been around half our lives, and we were somewhat used to seeing the soldiers about. The planes, however, were new to us. We had never seen anything like this before.

Then we saw the German tanks as they came clanking down the middle of the street, each one bearing a flag with the German swastika on it. They looked like huge metal beasts and made a noise that made us cover our ears.

Behind the tanks came the soldiers. They wore brownish-green uniforms and looked like a huge army of ants, with steel helmets covering their large, round heads. They had rifles hanging from their shoulders and shiny boots that were nearly as tall as we were. They marched like wind-up toys, kicking their legs high in the air, their boots drumming the ground.

An unusually large group of townspeople had gathered on the sidewalks and we wiggled our way through them. To our surprise, the Danish police officers of the town just stood by, looking at the parade with the rest of the people. Hanne and I huddled close, frightened by the terrible noise and the crowd of people that had gathered. We didn't know what to think.

As we watched, three soldiers approached the sidewalk, shoving their way through the people. One bulky soldier forced his way up to the fruit stand outside the grocery store and grabbed all the grapes he could hold in his hands. Laughing, he tossed the fresh fruit to other German soldiers who were not marching. Some missed the toss and the grapes fell to the ground to be instantly crushed by the shiny boots stamping down the street. Puzzled, I glanced at Hanne, I knew they had not paid for the produce.

Directly behind me in the crowd that had gathered, I heard our landlady say, "Johna, her mother, and Mrs. Johnsen, are the only Jews in this neighborhood. They really stand out, with their dark hair and eyes. The Germans have been talking a lot about the Jews, lately," she said.

She was using the tone of voice I recognized from the laundry room, when the women talked about their neighbors who weren't there.

I couldn't think what this meant, or what it had to do with the soldiers and tanks. I wondered if she were one my father's friends, and why she would care that my mother and I were Jewish. Most of our neighbors weren't Jewish, but until that moment, I never thought my being a Jew was of interest to anyone. The synagogue and my Jewish grandparents were one part of my life, and my Danish family and neighbors were another. That was just how life was, and it had not been worth noticing the difference. My father told me I was half-Danish, the good half, the Viking half. My mother and her father told me I was all Jewish. Rather than be confused, I simply hadn't thought about it at all.

Also behind me in the crowd stood Peter Dam, a fourth grader from school. Peter had dirty hair and wore wrinkled clothes. He was the school bully. He always said bad things about me and would grab my doll away from me. I tried to stay as far away from him as I could. Hanne and I saw him steal an apple and stuff it in his pocket.

"Why are they marching today?" I asked Hanne in a quiet

voice. "Is it for our King Christian? I heard he fell off his horse, Jubelee, at Amalienborg Castle and broke his leg."

In a flash Peter bolted in front of me, with his mouth still full of a bite of the apple he had stolen. He yelled into my face, "Can't you see it is a parade for the Germans who don't like Jewish girls with one hand and stupid eyeglasses?"

I could only stare at him. I didn't understand what he meant either. What did my arm or that I wore glasses have to do with anything? And what difference did it make that I was all or half Jewish?

The grocer who looked like Laurel pushed Peter away and grabbed the apple from his hand. Then the grocer we called Hardy, knelt down in front of me. I could smell the garlic on his breath.

"Men in German uniforms are bad!" he said. "They could hurt you, so stay away from them. Do you understand me, Johna?" He shook me for emphasis. "Go home now and don't play on the way!"

I nodded suddenly shy because he was so stern. Peter stood near, listening with a cruel smirk on his pimply face.

Hardy growled at us, "Go home now!" he said. "Run as fast as you can!" Hardy knew what Hanne and I could not—that something had changed in our country.

Hanne and I did as he said. We turned and ran toward home. Soon the sounds of the tanks and the marching faded behind me, but Peter's harsh words and the grocer's fierce warning still echoed in my head.

We ran on through the side streets until we reached the rear entry of my apartment on Sylviavej Street. Hanne pushed open the heavy wooden door into the tunnel that led to our backyard. I stood panting, trying to catch my breath. When I had rested enough, we skipped up the back stairs—she to her apartment on the third floor, me to mine on the second floor. I burst through the door into the kitchen.

"Who is chasing you that you are in such a state and all sweaty?" my mother asked. I called her Mor, which is Danish for mother.

"Oh, Mor, Laurel and Hardy weren't funny today," I told

her. "Hardy told me to run home as fast as I could, because there were mean Germans who could hurt me. The Germans were having a parade, and soldiers were everywhere."

Without a word, Mor gently pushed me toward my father, who was sitting at the kitchen table. I called him Far, which is Danish for father. I spilled out my story to him about the tanks in the street, the soldiers with their guns and their shiny boots. I told him how Peter had stolen an apple—just like the German soldier had stolen the grapes—right in front of everyone, and of the landlady who was talking about Mor and me being Jewish.

He listened to me in silence, and then said, "Calm down. Don't worry about Peter or any of this. The Germans are just showing off, having a little fun and playing a game. The soldiers are acting like bullies, just like Peter. Ignore them. Try hard not to be afraid. After all, you are my brave girl."

He handed me a *Film Star* magazine and told me to go lie on the big bed in the bedroom. I took the magazine and settled onto the bed. Thoughts of tanks and planes gave way as I looked at the pictures of my favorite movie stars, Tarzan and Rita Hayworth. Mor and Far continued to talk in low tones in the other room.

Mor's name was Jette Malka Pressmann Christensen, though Far only called her Margit. She was Jewish. Her father was a tailor who had come to Denmark from Russia when he and his first family had fled from a pogram there in 1906. His wife had died during their escape, and he had later remarried. My mother was born to his second wife.

I inherited my black curly hair from Mor, and she had dark brown eyes. Like her father, she knew how to sew and made all our clothes. She even knit clothes for my favorite dolly, whom I had named Jette, after her.

Besides the many things she did for us, she loved music and she and I had fun singing Jewish and Danish songs and dancing together. She was always humming a tune, carrying music inside her like a friend. She even played the piano at the Jewish community center.

Far was my father, but we didn't move in with him until I was three years old, and Mor was twenty-four. It wasn't until then that my Jewish grandfather had finally given his permission for them to marry. He had been unhappy that Mor had fallen in love with, and then gotten pregnant by, someone outside her faith. Mor felt his disapproval deeply, and felt she had dishonored her parents by getting pregnant, and so wouldn't do so further by marrying Far without her father's consent. He finally gave it when I was two, but it was in so off-hand a way that he never actually blessed their marriage.

Far and Mor married shortly after she and I moved in, and Mor worked hard to learn how to be a good Danish wife. She even learned to cook Danish food from my father's sisters because she wanted to please him so.

One thing she could not do, however, was give up her religion. Though she never complained about eating ham or Far's favorite pork dishes, she told me not to tell my grandfather about it. It was our secret, she said. She and I still attended synagogue services twice a month and on special Jewish holidays, even though it obviously annoyed my father. Far did not believe in church or synagogue. He thought her faith was a weakness and often told her so.

Far was Danish. His name was Poul Villy Christensen. He was named for my Danish grandmother, Poula, who ran a tavern in Copenhagen. He had piercing hazel eyes that didn't seem to blink. A stare from him would send shivers down my spine and frighten me into complete obedience. He wore his brown wavy hair slicked back with shiny lotion. He had a boyish face, and ladies always liked him, called him "cute," and said he was "so handsome." A carpenter by trade, he wore special white pants, with a white vest and a white captain's hat when he went to work. He smelled of lumber and sawdust. At that time, he was twenty-nine years old and a master carpenter—and proud of it. He was also proud of his Viking ancestry, though he had little use for its traditions. The only traditions that mattered to him were those of his trade.

When he was not at his job, however, he would dress in a fancy suit, vest, overcoat, and brim hat, looking more like an American banker than a Danish master carpenter. A big cigar usually hung from his mouth, and he smelled not of wood then, but the good cologne he wore. Far was a strong man, with strong ways. He expected things of me and I wanted to please him. He didn't allow crying and always told me I had to be strong and brave. Sometimes, though, it was hard. But he also took good care of me. He built me a nice dollhouse with my name on the roof. He would play a fun game with me, too. Sitting me on his lap facing him, he would jump his knees up and down and sing about a horse. Then he would widen his legs and I would fall between his knees while he held onto my arms, leaving me laughing.

Mor and Far came from two completely different worlds and though Mor wanted Far to enter hers, he never would. She would ask him to come with us to visit her parents, but he rarely did. When he did come, he and my Jewish grandfather and he normally ended up shouting at one another until one, or the other, stormed out of the room.

Mor would often ask Far to make peace with my grandfather.

"Never!" he would yell. One time during a fight I heard him yell, "I hate the Jews and their backward ways and foolish traditions!" Mor had shouted back that he only hated them because they had rejected him.

Just as Far would not really enter Mor's world, neither did he let her enter his. When he went out, or went to visit his mother's tavern, he went alone. Sometimes he took me to the tavern, but he left Mor at home when he did. Sometimes when he and Mor had a fight, he would leave and might not come back for a couple of days. Far took care of us, but he did so on his own terms.

That evening after dinner, Far said to me, "Johna, you must be brave like me and not a scared, stupid little girl like your mother, afraid of everything. Remember the time when you were afraid of the Halloween mask, and I placed an ugly mask at the end of your bed to teach you to be brave?"

"Ja, but I didn't like it, and couldn't fall asleep," I said.

Mor, who came to my aid when she thought Far was too harsh, quickly interrupted and changed the subject. "How about a warm tub bath tonight?" she asked.

She put the big metal tub in front of the hot coal stove in the living room. I was soon out of my clothes and with one foot at a time, I settled into the lukewarm water. Mor came from the kitchen with more hot water and carefully poured it into the tub. It felt good and I wiggled my toes, creating small ripples in the bath water. I pretended to be a mermaid, just like the statue in the harbor from the fairy tale by Hans Christian Andersen.

The living room smelled of Far's pipe tobacco. Seated in his brown leather chair, he scraped the old tobacco out of his pipe bowl. The large blue veins on the back of his hands resembled branches of a tree. As I watched him, I wished I had two strong hands like him, and had not been born with my left hand missing.

"Far, why don't I have a real hand and arm?" I asked him. He got up from his chair, came over to the tub and kissed my stub. He patted me on the head, but he did not answer me. I wanted to know why I had an arm that was so different, but I hardly ever asked because neither of my parents would ever answer me. It was years before I was to know that Mor had been troubled with morning sickness when she was pregnant with me and the doctor had given her a drug later known for the birth defects it caused.

Mor came out from the kitchen with more hot water for my bath. She poured it in, then sat down in her rocking chair. Sitting there in my warm bath, with Far smoking his pipe, and Mor rocking back and forth, made me feel safe. The events of the day faded away and I grew drowsy.

Then I overheard my parents talking about the Germans, and people called Nazis. They spoke of Jews being arrested, and said that even King Christian had been arrested.

"Poul, are Jews in danger—my parents perhaps? Johna and I?" Mor asked. "Have you heard what is going on?"

"We are all Danes and there is no danger I know of right now. The Germans have worked with Denmark for four years and have let us go about our business as usual. That's the way it's been until their elite army came in. Now some things are stirring. Some say they want complete control of our government and the Danish citizens, but I'm sure it is just a rumor. You and Johna are not Jews anymore since your father said I could marry you, and damn it," he said, anger touching his voice, "that was three years ago. Now you have the Danish name of Christensen. Don't be such a worry wart!"

"I am not a Jew anymore, Far?" I asked. He looked over at me and grinned.

"Do not worry Little Skat," he said. Little Skat was his nickname for me, and when he used it, it meant I was his little sweetheart. "The bad Germans will not do anything to you as long as I am around."

"How do you know so much about who is safe or not?" Mor asked.

"I don't want to discuss this subject anymore!" Far said, lifting a glass of whiskey to his mouth, and both Mor and I knew what that meant. Mor picked me up from the tub, gave Far a towel and put me in his lap. He rubbed me dry and kissed me on the forehead, then handed me back to Mor.

We all shared the one bedroom in our little apartment. Mor and Far's bed was against the wall, and my small bed stood closest to the window. After I put on my nightclothes, Mor tucked my bed quilts around me. Then we said our nightly prayer:

> *Oh God, I shut my eyes.*
> *In peace again, I hope to rise.*
> *While I take my nightly rest,*
> *Be with those I love the best.*
> *Guide me in thy holy way,*
> *Make me better every day.*
> *Shema, Israel Adonai,*
> *Elohainu Adonai, Echod.*
> *Hear, Oh Israel, the Lord our God,*
> *The Lord is One.*

Then she finished our nightly routine saying as she always did, "Peek-a-boo, I see you! Sleep good." Mor left the room, but left the bedroom door open behind her.

The day had given me a lot to think about. As I lay there, trying to sort it all out, I could hear my parents arguing about what the day's events meant. Suddenly I heard Far open the coat closet and Mor's voice raise.

"Go to your friends, then, and your Nazi meetings!" she screamed at Far.

"Don't talk back to me, Margit, I will do what I want!" he snapped back.

"Why can't you call me Malka or Jette, my real names?"

"Because those are Jew names, and you are now a Dane. Why can't you get that through your head?" Far was angry.

"No! No! I am a Jew and I always will be, and so is Johna!" Mor screamed back.

"Johna is only half Jewish," Far corrected her. "Being Jewish is just a silly religion anyway," he said.

"Papa says she is all Jewish because I'm a Jew. Race is not a religion."

"So? She is also Danish, and that makes her all Danish. Stop this foolish talk and shut up about this half and half," Far said.

I heard the front door slam. Mor came back to the bedroom. She was crying and dropped onto her bed. Neither of us spoke.

It was a long time before I fell asleep. So many sharp memories pinched me and chased away sleep. Finally it came to me, but it was uneasy. I dreamed of the gray shadows of tanks looming out of the darkness, the haunting sounds of marching German soldiers, and of the grocery man yelling at me to run.

In the middle of the night I woke to the smell of Far's beer breath. He stood over my bed, holding a cone filled with ice cream topped with whipped cream and jam.

"You're drunk," Mor yelled at him from the bed. "Leave her alone and let her sleep...It is three o'clock in the morning!"

Far ignored her and handed me the ice cream cone. Then he left the room, to return a moment later with a glass of milk that smelled of whiskey.

"Here's another treat," Far said, as he took the ice cream away from me. Still half asleep, I had let it drip all over me. He wiped up the drippy mess from the ice cream with his handkerchief. I stared at the hanky. It was white, and had a dainty trim sewn around the edges in blue thread. In the corner was an embroidered swastika, just like the ones I had seen on the German flags, on the sides of the tanks, on the German uniforms. I knew it was not Mor's.

Far saw my eyes and quickly returned the hanky to his pocket. He lifted the milk brew to my lips, and my insides warmed as the whiskey went down. I slid back under my comforter and this time, with Far home again, sleep came easily.

Chapter 2

More Changes

The next morning was Sunday. As soon as I woke up, I dressed and rushed to our front door to see if the Kringle Bakery had delivered the usual crispy rolls they always did on Sunday mornings. How I looked forward to those rolls, still warm from the oven. We ate them drizzling with butter, marmalade, and extra-sharp cheese. I opened the door, but nothing was there. I went to the living room window and looked out on the street, but it was empty. No one was even walking to the corner news-stand for the morning paper.

"Mor," I yelled toward the kitchen, "did the rolls come?"

"I will fix you some oatmeal today," said Mor, ignoring my question. Go take the garbage out while I get it ready." Mor motioned to the bag as I entered the kitchen. Carrying the gar-bage, I descended the green curved stairs into the back court-yard. Far was in the bicycle shed repairing the lock on the door, and I waved to make him think I liked taking out the garbage. I hated doing it. I hated the smell and was frightened of the rats that lived in the garbage bins, but I didn't want Far to know I was afraid.

Far just looked at me, and then went right on working. I shuffled my feet slowly toward where the garbage bin was en-closed by a wooden fence. Holding my breath against the smell, I stood on my tiptoes to unlatch the gate. Three rats stared over the fence at me, hissing and squeaking through their teeth. They scattered and scurried between my feet. I screamed at the top of my lungs.

"The rats, the rats!" I yelled, and jumped up and down and waved my arms, dropping the garbage bag as I did so.

"Johna, what in the hell's the matter with you? You are acting just like Mor. You are bigger than these rats, so shut off your fear," Far demanded. He reached down and picked up the bag.

"But look, Far, I'm not even crying!" I said.

"You have to shut off your feelings—just like when Peter teased you about your hand. If something bothers you, hide it."

"Yes, Far," I said, though I had no idea how to do what he said.

He tossed the garbage bag into the bin. When we turned to leave, a man in a black German uniform stood in our path, a bag of garbage in his hand.

"I heard a scream. What's going on?" The German soldier said. Behind him was Bente, a woman from our apartment complex. I often saw her at my Danish grandmother's tavern, the Absalon, drinking and partying with German soldiers. She was pretty and looked like my favorite movie star, Rita Hayworth.

"What are you doing here?" Far asked him, his voice sharp.

"Is that any of your business?" said the German, with just as much of an edge to his voice.

"Johna, go home to Mor!" Far said.

As I left, the German put his hand on my sleeve.

"Where do you live, little girl? You sure have pretty dark curls!"

"She is my daughter, why do you want to know?" I heard Far say as I ran off.

"Don't run away, I don't bite!" the soldier shouted after me.

Back in the apartment, I told Mor about the German in the courtyard and how he frightened me. She went to the window and leaned close to the glass, the moisture from her breath clouding the window. Footsteps sounded on the stairs outside our apartment. I froze and waited, afraid it might be the German coming, but it was only Far. He gave me an angry look and I knew he was not happy that my screaming had drawn the attention of the soldier.

"Who was that, Poul?" Mor asked.

"A Kraut! A German piece of shit. An SS officer—of Hitler's *elite*, with a skull-and-crossbones insignia on his uniform. He was visiting that whore, Bente, downstairs. I will tell her a thing or two as soon as I see her again!" he bellowed.

"Don't start, Poul. You'll put us in the middle. She may know something about us that we may regret, with things like they are. Let's go see if my parents are all right, and find out what they have heard of the Jews being in danger," Mor said.

"We are not going to your father's house," he said. "I ran into your brother yesterday, and he told me they were all fine. Your father only tolerates me, and I don't like the old apartment they live in with its faded curtains. The old man smells, the old woman smells, and the kitchen smells. It stinks like a museum. The whole place reeks of boiled chicken and the oily smoke of those old candles. For God's sake, I can't even get a glass of beer. He is stubborn in his foolish religion and refuses to speak Danish when I am around just to piss me off. He gets on my nerves. He would not let me help anyhow, that's for sure."

"You just dislike my parents because you don't understand Jewish ways," Mor said.

"Damn right! I have good reason. Now just leave me alone!" Far pushed Mor out of his way and sat down to the paper from the day before.

Mor motioned me to come and sit with her on the green couch. She combed my hair while I held a hand mirror to watch what she was doing.

"Look, Johna, how little your cute nose is on your face, it's not a Jewish nose!" Mor said to me.

"Far, what is a Jewish nose?" I asked, disturbing him from his reading. He peeked over the top of the newspaper up at me.

"Ask your Jewish grandfather!" he said with a laugh.

When Far said that it made me think of my Jewish grandfather, Yechiel Pressmann. I called him Zayde because that was the Jewish name for "grandfather." He was shorter than most men. He had a bulky body, a fat belly, dark brown eyes, and gray hair that peeked out from under his yarmulke, the little round hat he always wore. He always smelled of clean soap and mothballs, and his mustache and beard would tickle me when he kissed and hugged me.

Unlike Far, who wore two different kinds of clothes, Zayde only wore suits and vests, with a pocket watch and chain hanging from the buttonhole of his vest. And best of all, Zayde always had wrapped candy in his suit pocket.

Like Mor, Zayde also loved music. He had a loud voice, and he taught me many Jewish songs to sing while he played his violin. He also taught me to dance, and would play games with me, like spinning the dreidel for Hanukkah, as well as many others. As a tailor, he sewed uniforms for mailmen and the Danish Police. He even made me a blue coat with shiny gold buttons from the leftover cloth. Zayde liked to read, and told me many stories from the Old Testament of the Bible. He let me drink wine in my very own tiny goblet on special Jewish holidays. The best place for me when I was sad, was on Zayde's lap. I loved Zayde, and could not understand why Far did not.

"Johna," Far said, "you and I will go to a soccer game. Soccer's a mean game, and the players are brave. Brave people don't scream or cry when they're afraid or hurt. They do what must be done, rats or no rats. That's life." He watched Mor combing my tangled curls.

Suddenly, he bolted out of his chair, threw his wrinkled newspaper on the floor, and went to the window.

"Damn it!" Far said, looking at something outside.

I followed him to the window to see what it was that upset him. I saw a huge German tank parked at the end of our street. The soldiers were shooing away crowds of curious children. Neils Strum, the policeman who lived below us, directed bike traffic around the tank. Without a word, Far left the apartment, slamming the door behind him. I watched from the window as he went down to the street where he joined the others gathered around the German tank.

"Mor...is Far mad at us?" I asked, thinking of how I had screamed over the rats.

"No, Johna," she said, then stopped. She struggled to talk for a moment or two, but then said nothing more.

It was two days before Far came home, and Kringle's Bakery never delivered hot rolls again.

Chapter 3

Stolen Names

When I was not playing with Hanne or my dollhouse in those days, I'd often play a pretend game with the little figures on the hand-carved front of our cedar chest. The chest had been a gift to Far from a German soldier friend, Alfred, who would meet Far at my Danish grandmother's tavern. It was a large chest, about three feet high and almost five feet long. Mor kept her linens in it, and it sat right next to my dollhouse in our living room.

I liked the chest. The carving on the front portrayed ten men sitting at tables holding up beer steins in a salute. To me they had looked like Vikings sitting around wooden tables and reminded me of Far and his friends when they drank at my Danish grandmother's tavern in Copenhagen. I would talk to the figures as if I were in a theater, pretending they came alive and told me stories of their adventures.

After the day the tank appeared on our street and the rolls weren't delivered, however, my game changed. I saw the figures as Germans and I would tell them to go away. Far came in one time and overheard me when I was playing. He laughed and immediately told the Germans on the chest to be nice to me.

One Saturday morning, about three weeks after the tank had appeared on our street, Far came into the living room where I was playing my game with the chest.

"Johna, if you put a sugar cube in the window, the stork might stop and leave us a baby!" Far said.

It was folklore among the Danes and other Northern European countries that babies were brought by the beautiful storks that were common in the countryside, lore that also migrated to America. One would see their huge nests in the chimneys of farmhouses, where the heat would warm their eggs. It was an equally old practice to entice the stork to pay a visit by putting a lump of sugar in the window.

"What stork from the farm houses' roofs would remember

to fly by and deliver it to us?" I asked. I had not seen many storks in our area, so it seemed to me that sugar must not always work. "And if it does, when will the stork come?" I asked, jumping up and down at the idea of a new brother or sister.

"It will take about seven more months," Mor said, looking up from her knitting.

"Can I have a sugar cube to put in the window for the stork?" I asked Mor, suddenly very eager to get this business started.

"Oh, Johna," she laughed, "we need to talk about this later. A baby isn't exactly brought by a stork."

I couldn't think what Mor meant. Far had told me the stork would bring a baby. So had my teacher. I ran and got a sugar cube myself and then put it on the windowsill above my bed, while Mor and Far followed me, laughing at my excitement.

"I'll check it every day until we get a baby," I said. Then I had a thought. "Far, will the baby have only one hand like me?" I asked.

"Don't wish that. That's a bad thing to wish for," he said with some force. He shook his head so hard he spilled his beer. Confused, I hid my short arm behind my back, and wondered why he thought my hand was a bad thing. It was just like my having to wear eyeglasses was bad. These were new thoughts for me. Before it had just been the way I was, not anything special. Not good, not bad, just me. But in recent days I had had these things mentioned in ways that made me feel different because of them. For the first time, I began to feel shame.

"The stork will be a long time coming," Mor told me, but I saw her look at Far as if she were asking him a question.

"I don't care," I said. "Every time he flies over our house he will see the sugar cube and be reminded we want him to stop."

"You plan well ahead, little one," Far said. His voice was softer, but he didn't look at me. Then, as was his way, his mood shifted. "Johna would you like a brother...or maybe a sister?" he asked me.

"A sister," I started to say, but Mor answered before I could, her eyes again on Far.

"God will decide for us, we can only wait," she said.

Far tightened his jaw, his eyes narrowed. "Did your God

choose Johna to be born the way she was, is that how your God treats his people?" he said, quick to challenge Mor's faith whenever he could.

Zayde always said, "The Almighty is the Almighty, and He will do what He will do." Far, on the other hand, expected God to behave with reason and to want the best for his people. It made no sense to him that an all-powerful being should allow so many bad things to happen to people. It made him only feel contempt for Zayde and his passive acceptance of the Almighty's ways.

"Please, Poul, can't we just enjoy this new baby without arguing?" Mor said. Then she turned to me. "It is Saturday synagogue service today, Johna. Go get on your shoes and blue coat."

Far said nothing more, so I ran to get ready.

The weather was rainy and dark as we took a trolley to the underground Klampenborg train station. When we entered the station to get our tickets, I saw German soldiers standing guard on the station platforms, watching the people come and go. Every now and then they would stop a few of the passengers to talk with them. I stared at them, wondering what they were saying to those people.

"Don't look at the soldiers, Johna," said Mor, moving closer to me and holding my hand tight. I stared at the ground. This, too, was new to me. The last time we'd gone to synagogue, there hadn't been any German soldiers. I could hear the soldiers' boots tap and click behind us as they walked past where we waited for our train. It made me afraid. To my relief, they did not come to talk to us, and at last our train came.

When we reached our stop, the train door opened and we got off. Mor and I then walked the few blocks to Krystalgade Avenue, past the synagogue to the Jewish Senior Center apartments where my grandparents lived. Leaving Mor behind, I ran ahead down the long hall to their apartment and its unlocked door. I burst in and found my grandfather playing his violin and sitting as usual and in his favorite blue overstuffed chair, with the faded white doilies on its fat arms.

Happy to see him, I bounced up on his lap before he hardly had time to put down the violin. He gave me a hug and kissed me. I reached into his vest pocket to pull out his watch to listen to its steady tick-tock. Zayde reached into his other vest pocket and pulled out some coins and handed them to me.

"Thank you, BedsteFar," I said. His legs jerked suddenly, and I almost fell off his lap.

"*Zayde* is my name to you, Johna," he said in loud, broken Danish. "'BedsteFar' is Danish for Grandfather. You are *Jewish* in my house! Your mother is a Jew and that makes you a Jew. Your father is a Dane, and he can't be a Jew. We are Jews, and we can never *not* be Jews— no matter where we live!"

His outburst frightened me and I squirmed free from his lap and ran to my grandmother. I couldn't understand why he was so angry, why this business of Jewish and not Jewish, Danish and not Danish was so important to everyone.

My Bubbe, which was Jewish for "grandmother," scooped me into her arms. Her name was Brochr Miriam. She was tall compared to Zayde, and wore round glasses so thick I could not tell the color of her eyes. She wore heavy gold earrings that made her ear lobes look too long. Her hair, long and black with gray streaks, hung down past her waist. She always wore it braided and piled high in a bun on the back of her head. She wore long-sleeved blouses, and skirts that reached to her shoes. She smelled like sweet talcum powder and was always humming a song to herself.

Bubbe liked to cook. When we visited, she would let me help her make the braided bread called *challah*, which we ate with *gefilte* fish and horseradish mustard. She would fry potato cakes called *latkes*, and serve them along with good chicken soup or with Matzo balls that smelled of garlic and browning fat from the frying pan. We'd drink hot tea together in tall glasses while we cooked. After she had all the food ready and on the table, she would cover everything with cloth napkins. Then Zayde would say several Berakhah prayer blessings. Usually by the time he finished, the food would be cold.

As Bubbe hugged me, Mor came into the apartment.

"Johna," she said, with a smile on her face, "tell Bubbe what you put on the windowsill over your bed!"

"A sugar cube, for the stork!" I said, and looked back and forth between Zayde and Bubbe to see what they thought of this.

Zayde looked at Bubbe.

"Oh, Malka," she said, sighing. "Oh, Malka."

"What is 'Oh, Malka'?" Zayde asked her.

"The stork, Zayde," I repeated. "The stork is bringing a baby to our house!"

"The stork," he said, turning to me and smiling. He rose up and hugged my mother. "The good book in the Talmud Tora says that the stork has a lovely name called Chasidah," said Zayde. "That means 'the loving one,' and that is because it cares so much for its own mate and babies."

"Is it a kosher stork, Zayde?" I asked.

He laughed then, and came over to tickle me. "The stork only gives warmth to its own, like I give to you, little Johnalee," he said. Then he stopped and looked at his pocket watch.

"Come, put on your coats; it is time to go. What a fine evening to go to the synagogue," he said as he readied himself to leave.

A light mist was still coming down as we walked to the short distance to the synagogue. Once there, we entered and passed into the enormous interior where pillars rose to high ceilings painted in white and gold. In the center of the synagogue, lamps hung from the balcony that lined the side of the room, casting a warm yellow light over the area below. Mor, Bubbe, and I always sat in the balcony. The men always gathered on the main floor, where a large gilded Menorah candelabra stood wrapped in the glow of its own light. An elaborate ark sat at the front of the synagogue. This would open during the service, showing the Tora behind a glass window. Soon after we settled in our places in the balcony, Rabbi Milcher began the cantor prayers to thank God for all his goodness. The Rabbi was tall and wore glasses. He wore a hat that stood even taller, making his head look small and his ears look huge where they stuck out from under it. The sight of him made me laugh to myself, and I wondered if Far would dare to make fun of a Rabbi.

I had been to the synagogue so many times that I chanted along in Yiddish just like everyone else. "Shaman O Israel! The Lord thy God is one. Thou shalt love the Lord thy God with all of thy heart and all of thy soul and all of thy might," the chant ran. I looked down from the balcony. Below me, Zayde, in his black skullcap and his black and white prayer shawl with fringed silk draped over his shoulders, rocked back and forth deep in prayer. I could not imagine Far doing such a thing.

After the service we went to a community room for dinner. We sat down at the table to eat, but the people around us were agitated and talking in anxious tones. We heard them say the German Army had broken into the synagogue during the night. They had taken cabinets and broken into the desks in the synagogue office. Important records had been stolen, they said, records that had the addresses of all the Jews listed in the synagogue registry.

I didn't know what this meant but as Mor heard the news, she stopped eating and her face grew white and still. Suddenly she stood up, pushed her chair back from the table, and grasped my hand. With food still in my mouth, Mor rushed me out the door and ran to the train station, half dragging me along. We didn't even stop at the Jewish café to eat dessert as we usually did. On the train, German soldiers walked up and down the aisles. I could feel how tense Mor was and only dared to look down at their wet boots. Outside, the rain was pouring down so hard we could not see through the train windows. We heard a loud, rumbling boom, and flashes of light slashed across the evening sky. It seemed to me as if my whole world were being slit in two by that light.

When Mor and I finally arrived home safely, we found Far listening to the radio. He just looked at us and said, "Where's my dinner, I'm hungry!"

"Poul," said Mor in a rush, "did you know the synagogue secretary's private office was broken into last night? The rumors are that the Germans stole the registration protocols of birth, weddings, and deaths of all the Jews in Copenhagen."

"So?" said Far.

"That list has the names and addresses of Jews who contribute money to the synagogues in Denmark, and their addresses," she said.

"So what?"

"Johna and I are on that list," Mor told him.

"You give money to the Synagogue?" Far said, his voice rising. He glared hard at her.

"No, No! But Papa does, and includes us in his giving!"

"Damn! I do not like this a bit," said Far, his eyes cold, jaw set. "I don't want those German bastards to know where I live, or know that I'm married to a Jew. The Nazi Party has changed for the worse. They think they are the 'perfect race' with only good genes, genes that do not make handicapped babies. If they knew I had a child that was not *perfect—and* a little Jewish!—they would not let me be a member." He paused, thinking hard. "This means I can't attend their meetings anymore." Then he snapped his paper and swore. "Damn! Damn it, Margie!"

"You are scaring me, Poul, what are you involved with?" Mor said, her face full of fear.

"That is not your business—it is man thing," said Far.

My mother's fear leapt across the room to me; Far's anger made me anxious. Trying to be included in their conversation, I piped up, "I'm afraid of the bad Germans, Far! Would they not like me?"

"Johna, shut up! Don't hang around when we're talking. Go play!"

Not knowing what else to do, I turned and went into the kitchen to get a drink of water. When I heard them go into the bedroom and shut the door, I came back into the living room and sat down by the cedar chest. I looked at the carved figurines I had been playing with only a short time ago and wondered why someone would steal names.

Chapter 4

Secrets

The following Monday morning school was closed for the day, and I was glad to have a day off just to play. I was lying in front of my doll house when Mor came out of the bedroom, her eyes puffy and red.

"Mor?" I asked.

"Yes, Johna?"

"Are you sick? You look sick..."

Mor gave me a small smile, but did not answer my question. Instead, she said, "Today we have to wash clothes or I will lose my turn in the laundry room. Come with me, Johna, and help me."

"Yes, Mor," I said, and we gathered up our things and put them in the big laundry basket. We started up the stairs to washroom located several floors above us in the loft at the very top of the building. Part way up the stairs I stopped. "Mor, I'm tired. My shoes are tired of climbing. I want to sit down and rest," I told her. To my surprise she stopped and sat down on the stairs.

"Yes," she said, "me, too."

We sat on the stairs a moment in silence, balancing the clothes basket between us. I watched her face, trying to understand what it was I felt. She turned to me.

"I'm fine, Johna," she said. "I just didn't sleep well last night."

I knew that was all the answer I was going to get. Soon we stood up and continued up the stairs, stopping every so often to rest. Finally, we reached the laundry room.

Inside, a large, round copper tub sat above a burner in the middle of the room. A drain in the white and gray tile floor beneath it carried away the dirty wash water. Mor picked up the long hose that lay nearby and filled the tub with water. Then she lit the gas flame underneath. I threw the clothes into the big tub while Mor mixed in the soap with a round wooden stick. I put the scrub board in the side of the tub and watched as Mor scrubbed Far's dirty work clothes over the steel ridges of the wooden washboard.

"This kettle is big enough to cook three bad Germans, isn't it?" I asked, thinking about things I had heard in the last week.

"What in the world made you say that?" asked Mor in surprise.

"Germans are bad. Hanne told me they were just like the little men in the cartoons with bones in their noses. They would cook people, she said, and they are the ones who should be cooked."

"Don't ever talk like that about people, Johna," Mor said, and swatted me hard on the leg. It stung me, and tears burned at the corners of my eyes. Everyone said the Germans were bad and I couldn't understand why I was punished for saying so. Mor must have seen my confusion, for she began to coax me into singing funny Jewish songs with her as we worked on the clothes.

While the clothes stewed a bit in the hot water, I took the stirring stick and rode it around like a horse while Mor worked on her knitting. When the clothes had boiled enough, Mor opened a tap near the bottom of the tub. Steaming water spewed out of the hole and spread over the sloping tile floor.

"Watch your feet, Johna!" Mor yelled at me. "Move or it will scald you!" I hopped out of the way.

The loft was not only where the laundry room was, but also where our neighbor across the hall from us, Steen Larsen, kept his homing pigeons. He raced his birds against those belonging to other pigeon owners to the tower next to Bispebjerg Hospital, launching them from our apartment loft. Just as Mor started to hang our clothes up in the drying area next to the washroom, Mr. Larsen appeared in the doorway.

"Hello Margit!" he said. "Not much mason work for me in this wet weather, so I thought I would clean up my cages. Can Johna come and help me?"

Mor smiled, and I knew that meant yes.

I turned and went with him. Mr. Larsen was a mason by trade, and often worked on construction jobs with Far. He had never married and lived alone. He always wore a black fisherman's cap set crookedly across his forehead, and had a red mustache that drooped over his lips. He had pink, round cheeks that made his nose look white, and his belly was so full and round it strained the buttons on his pants and shirt. He and Far often stopped after work at the Valby tavern to have a beer together.

As we climbed up a ladder to a platform where the cages sat, the scent of the feathers and droppings filled the air and I heard the sound of cooing. Mr. Larsen handed me a large sack of cracked corn and let me feed the beautiful birds. While I gave them fresh water, he told me pigeons were not like other birds that have to raise their heads up to swallow. I pulled out a white one and held it in my arms, stoking the soft feathers.

"Mr. Larsen, are the pigeons in the town square all yours? There are a lot of them there, and they jump on our hands when we have food for them."

"No, Johna, these are special messenger pigeons, and they always come back to their cage. Actually they are not really pigeons," he told me, "they are doves."

I liked the sound of that word. It was so much softer than 'pigeon.' "What do messenger pigeons—doves—do?"

"They carry mail to my friends. Look here," he said, and I watched while he fastened a small tube to one of the bird's legs. It looked like a tiny bracelet.

"Where will it go?" I asked.

"Wherever I tell it to. That's why they are so special," he said. "I train each of them to go only to one place...this one is going to the tower next to the hospital." Then he held the bird up and whispered to it to fly away.

We kept cleaning out the cages and putting fresh food and water in them. I heard something, and looked up just in time to see one of his gray birds trying to enter the cage from outside the window ledge.

"Mr. Larsen! One has come back, there!" I said, pointing.

"Come to me, little pigeon..." he said, speaking to the bird in a soft voice. He reached out and gently grabbed the pigeon in his hand. He turned the bird carefully over on its side and removed a little bracelet tube just like the one he had put on the other bird from this one's leg. He opened the tube and pulled a piece of rolled-up paper from it.

"What does it say?" I asked, hopping up and down in

eagerness. Mr. Larsen, a funny look on his face did not answer me. He looked into space the same way Far did sometimes. I picked up the small tube the message had come in and saw it had a red cross on it, just like what was on the side of ambulances. "Is it a letter?" I asked, thinking this was just like the postman.

"It's nothing, Johna," he said. "Nothing. We're all done here, so you go on now and help your mother. As I left I saw him write something on the paper with a stubby pencil. Then he put it in another bird's bracelet and released the new bird into the air.

I headed back down the ladder to the wash room. Mor was waiting for me and together we went back to our apartment. Both of us had wet hair from the steam in the laundry room, so Mor toweled my hair. When we were dry again, we left to go to the Valby Market to shop for the evening meal. At the market we found a long line of people waiting to get meat.

"I hear there is only hamburger and some pork left," the lady behind us said. "The Germans are rationing our food so they can send more to Germany. We Danes are given what's left of our own meat, and for that, we pay more and more."

I leaned into Mor and whispered, "Are we going to get hamburger or pork?"

"We will get what we can get," Mor said. When it was our turn at the counter, pork was all that was left.

That evening, Mor was preparing dinner when Far arrived home, smelling like sawdust and sweat. He sat down to eat before taking a shower. As we were cutting up our pork roast and potatoes covered with gravy, Far said with a smirk, "Aha! Margit you are learning to enjoy pork!"

Mor looked over at Far and threw her knife and fork down on the table, shoved her chair back, and stormed out of the room. Far watched Mor leave the kitchen, then as he reached for more roast pork, he winked at me across the table and smiled, a secret between us.

"Far?"

"Yes, Johna," he answered.

"Far, I helped feed Mr. Larsen's pigeons today, and guess what? They have round rings around their feet, with small tubes that have notes inside." I told Far about the beautiful birds and how they carried messages just like the postman did, thinking he would like them, too. To my surprise, he grew angry at me.

"Johna," said Far, sharp and strong, "this isn't a child's game! Mr. Larsen's pigeons are a secret, and you're not to tell anyone about them carrying mail. Do you understand?"

"Why Far?" I asked, my voice shaking. Mr. Larsen had not said they were a secret, but here was Far, angry at me for talking about them.

"It's not for you to ask. Just do as I say. If you tell Hanne or anyone else, bad things could happen."

"What kind of bad things?"

"Things like a spanking for you, if you tell anyone."

My mouth felt dry. I tried to swallow as I kept tears back and couldn't. Far saw them and his face changed. He leaned closer to me, took my shoulders in his hands.

"Listen, Johna," he said, giving me a soft squeeze, "if you don't tell anyone, that will make you a big girl, and you will be almost grown up." He smiled at me. "Understand?"

"OK," I said, nodding. "OK. I won't tell anyone."

"Good. This will be a real test for you. We'll keep this special secret, just between us, yes? Won't it be fun?" Far smiled at me again. Far's smiles could convince a six-year-old to do anything.

"All right, Far. Just you and me," I said, pointing first to his chest and then to my own. "I won't tell anyone about the messages the pigeons are carrying, I promise."

"Pigeons sending messages?" asked Mor, coming backing into the kitchen. "To whom?"

"I will tell you later, Margit. You get upset about every little thing."

Then Far smiled at me again and pulled me up onto his knees and bounced me, singing the horse song I so loved. He bounced me up and down, and when he pretended to drop me on the floor, I laughed and laughed. I loved it when Far played this with me. I was just about to asked him to do it again when there was a knock on our kitchen door. Far opened it and found Hanne there, carrying her napkin collection. She came in and we went into the other room where we played napkin trading.

This was a game we had between us, where each of us collected pretty napkins and then we would trade them back and forth between ourselves, and with other girls in our neighborhood, each trying to gather the best collection.

"If you give me two of your napkins, I will trade you for the 'dove' napkin you want," Hanne said.

"That's not fair," I said, but then I remembered I had a special reason now for wanting that napkin. "Oh, all right," I said, handing over the two in exchange. I wanted to tell Hanne why the napkin was so important to me, but if I wanted to be a big girl for Far, I knew I couldn't. I had to keep it a secret even from Hanne.

"Let's go and eat some of the cookies my mother made," Hanne said. "I have some new cartoons for you to see, too."

"Can I, Mor?"

"I will come up to get you when I want you to come home," Mor said, and Hanne and I left for her upstairs apartment.

Hanne's mother, Lillian, was a teacher at our school. She had lots of shelves filled with reading books, and under the coffee table we always found fashion magazines and other things to read that her mother had bought at the store. I read the new cartoons Hanne had for a while. Then I picked up a black book that was lying on top of the table.

"You want to look at the pictures in my mother's Bible?" Hanne asked, pointing to the book I held in my hand.

"Sure," I said, so we sat together on the sofa and thumbed through the pages. I saw a picture of a man with a halo on his head and angels coming down on beams of sunshine through the clouds. I had never seen this kind of picture before, and took the book from Hanne to look closer. Just then, my mother came to the door and spoke a moment with Mrs. Hansen. Then she turned to me.

"What are you looking at?" Mor asked, coming over to me. She took the book from me to see. Her face turned red and she dropped the book on the floor. Then she grabbed my arm and jerked me to a standing position. Mrs. Hansen stepped forward and picked up the black book.

"Margit, I know you are Jewish, but it is a harmless Bible and she is just a child. Don't be so upset," Hanne's mother said.

"Lillian, just do not interfere about my reasons and mind your own business," Mor blurted out. She pulled me across the room to the front door.

"Don't you ever again look in that black book," Mor said, spanking me hard on my thigh.

Her sudden anger brought tears to my eyes. Mrs. Hansen said nothing, but slammed the door shut behind us.

"Why can't I look in it? Hanne can!" I wailed.

"Zayde tells us that book is a fake, and it is not for Jews to look at or read. Just do what you are told and stop asking why all the time!" she snapped at me, her face still red. I had never seen my mother so angry at me before.

At home, my father had his nose in the food-cooling closet, searching for something to eat. He looked over at me and saw the unhappy look on my face.

"What's the matter with her, Margit?" Far asked.

"Nothing is wrong, Poul!" And to my relief Mor did not tell him about the book. If looking at it had made her that mad, I couldn't think what Far would do. First birds, now a book my world suddenly seemed full of traps for me.

Later that day, when it was almost dark, I was sitting at the kitchen table looking at my new white dove napkin when I heard an airplane overhead. Planes were not everyday things in our world then, and thinking of that day just a few weeks earlier, I ran to the window to see. Far and Mor reached it first. Together we leaned over and watched as hundreds of blue pieces of paper drifted to the pavement below. The wings of the plane flashed silver, bright sparks in the light of the lowering sun.

"Far, is it a German plane dropping paper? Are more tanks and more Germans coming?" I asked, my stomach suddenly uncomfortable.

"What? No, no. I think it's a British airplane...yes, it is!" Far said, jumping up. I didn't know what that meant, but his excitement caught me up and we all rushed down to the sidewalk where the neighbors had already gathered.

Blue papers were scattered all over our yard. Far bent over to pick up one of them up.

"What are they, Far? What do they say?" I asked.

"The leaflets describe how the British will be victorious over Nazi Germany," he explained. "The message urges us Danes to resist the Germans, to convince the rest of Europe that Denmark is only an occupied country, and not a friend of Hitler's."

"How could we resist Hitler's army, Poul? Are they crazy?" Mor asked.

"There are a lot of Danes, now, that are rebelling and will not stand the Germans telling us what we can and can't do, what we can buy, while they keep our food and bakeries to themselves. It is too much," he said, a small smile playing on his lips.

Back at the apartment Far paced the floor and peeked out the window from time to time.

"There are more Germans starting to gather on the street," he said. He turned back to the room, took a few more steps, then suddenly slammed his fist down on the table, shaking the dishes. "I'm going to the tobacco store and then to a Danish resistance meeting to discuss how this German occupation is getting worse. I don't know when I will be home."

"Be careful, Poul," Mor begged, for Far often left us for days without saying when he would come back. He would not tell us where he had been, and Mor knew that to ask was to invite his anger.

"*Ja! Ja!*" Far said as he went out the door, scarcely looking back at us.

The rest of the evening I organized my napkin collection, putting my new dove napkin on top of the pile, a reminder of the beautiful soft birds I'd seen that day and the secret I needed to keep.

Chapter 5

Nazis Crack Down

By the early fall of 1943, it was growing clear to the Nazis that Danish support for the Nazi party was dwindling. Not only that, but as the Nazis lost ground in other parts of Europe, the Danish underground resistance movement began to step up acts of sabotage. Public demonstrations grew larger, occurred more frequently. Hitler realized conciliation with the Danes wasn't going to work and he would have to take a tougher stand in our tiny country. All of this, however was well over Hanne's and my heads. Over the next few days after Far left, Hanne and I played together whenever we could, whispering to one another about the day blue papers had fallen fluttering from the sky. Far came and went, came and went, flickering into our lives and then disappearing again. Every night, Mor cried.

I didn't know what to think of her crying, for Far always told me, "Only small babies cry," and was angry whenever I did. It didn't make sense to me, for Mor was a woman, not a baby, and she was my mother. It seemed somehow that she would be stronger than me, and it frightened me to hear her weeping. If I asked her what was wrong, she just told me to never mind.

In spite of the theft of the lists of people's names from the synagogue, Zayde still insisted Mor and I come twice a month for synagogue and for every Jewish holiday. This had to have been hard for my mother. She believed so strongly that a woman should obey and support her husband, but she also believed in honoring her father. She was perhaps driven by her own sense of shame over first getting pregnant by, and then marrying, a gentile. This kept her moving back and forth between two very different worlds

Many times Mor tried to merge the two, but they refused to be reconciled. She always asked Far to go to my grandparents' home with us, but he seldom agreed. On occasions when he did accompany us, he and Zayde invariably ended up shouting at one another, and one or the other would storm out of the apartment. One time as we were leaving, I heard her tell Far under her breath, "I should have had Johna by a Jewish man. Not a damn Dane." I don't remember what Far said back, but I do remember wondering what she meant. A Jewish father? What did that mean? I couldn't imagine a different far than Far and it hurt me to even think of it.

One Monday after school Hanne and I were playing in the backyard of our apartment building with a group of other neighborhood children. Though it was barely raining, Hanne carried her red umbrella anyway. She was proud of its bright color and stylish appearance. I thought it was the most beautiful thing I had ever seen. Of course, I wanted one just like it, though I would never admit that to Hanne. Instead, I ran up the stairs to get Far's plain black umbrella. I hurried back down to the yard and opened it wide as I came out the door.

"This one is much better than your stupid red umbrella," I told Hanne, full up to my eyes with envy, "It's bigger and keeps more rain off me, not like a little red 'toy' umbrella." As I bragged, a gust of wind snatched the big umbrella right out of my hand and sent it tumbling across the courtyard.

Hanne only laughed, ignored me, and started singing one of our favorite songs. She and another girl, Lise, sat in a wooden boat Far had brought home. He had built it for the Tivoli Gardens amusement park, which had a small lake in it where they rented boats for people to use. I was proud that Far had a boat from Tivoli Gardens. I climbed in with them, umbrellas forgotten, and we pretended we were Vikings sailing across the sound to Sweden.

Suddenly a loud noise interrupted us.

"What's that noise?" Lise asked.

"It's so loud. Where's it coming from?" I asked.

Hanne jumped out of the boat. "We have to go...look!" she said, pointing to the apartment building. Lise and I looked up and saw our mothers waving to us from our apartment windows. We realized then that the sound we heard was that of everyone's radio turned up and blaring out the windows. Lise and I jumped out of the boat and ran after Hanne.

As soon as I entered our apartment, Mor told me to sit on

a footstool and be quiet. "Don't move from that footstool and don't speak," she said, sounding as stern as Far. I wondered what I had done wrong this time, why I had to come in.

To my surprise I saw our upstairs neighbor, Mrs. Johnsen, sitting on the couch. She was a good friend of Mor's and often took care of me when Mor and Far would go out dancing. I liked her. She was soft and round, and would hold me on her lap. Like me, she was also half Jewish. Zayde would say she was *all* Jewish, not half. And like Zayde, she had also fled Russia, but a little later than he had. She came in 1916, the same year Mor was born. She didn't go to synagogue, but she had cousins in Copenhagen who did.

I looked to the other side of the room and saw Far was home. He was standing with two of his friends beside the radio. On one side was his Swedish friend, Thor Pehrssen, who was an architect Far had met through work. Since Far was a master carpenter, the two spent many evenings together going over drawings of buildings he was going to build. Thor often crossed the sound to Sweden in his own motorboat to visit his family in Aesthete and sometimes he took us along for three-day vacations in Sweden.

On the other side of the radio was Far's friend Erik Olsen. He had thick blond hair, pretty white teeth, and big blue eyes. He was the kind of man that women loved and men envied for his carefree life-style and his way with women. When Erik came into a room, everyone noticed. He always looked good, wearing white starched shirts with fancy suspenders and fine looking suits. He smelled good, too, of musk cologne.

Erik did not work at a job the way Far did, but he never seemed short of money. This combination sometimes led to bouts with the police. They would occasionally put him in jail and Far would have to bail him out. The truth was Erik lived on the edge of legality, sometimes stealing or smuggling, or perhaps fencing someone else's stolen goods.

These things didn't mean anything to me. All I knew was that he was handsome and always wanted me to call him by his first name, unlike any other adult in my world. He went out of his way to be nice to Mor and I and would often chat with us, telling us funny stories to make us laugh. That was how his charm worked; he was warm, friendly, knew what would please you and would give it. Sometimes I wished Far could be more like Erik.

Mor said Erik's blue eyes and smile would melt the heart of any girl. That seemed to be true, for he had brought any number of young women to our apartment, though it was never the same one twice. She pretended to disapprove of his activities. "It is not right the way Erik buys stolen goods and sells them on the black market," Mor would say to Far. But then Erik gave her two mink coats as gifts, and it was hard to complain about that.

Erik and Far had been best friends since they were school boys in the neighborhood. Mor said they had both been hooligans. Far would brag that whenever they would get up to something, Erik would always be the one to get caught, while Far would always get away. Erik, he said, just wasn't fast enough. The police usually just gave him a warning, though, and let him go. Even they were not immune to his charm and easy nature.

One time, a long time before the tanks and soldiers came, Erik and Far had gone to the racetrack. When Mor and I came home from grocery shopping, and started to climb the stairs, we came across piles of horse poop on the steps. We looked at one another in surprise, wondering how horse poop could have gotten on the stairs of our apartment building.

When we reached our apartment I headed for the bathroom. When I opened the bathroom, door, I looked straight into the rear end of a horse. I screamed and tried to close the door. Mor came running to see what was the matter and she saw the same horse hind end that I had.

"How in the world did he get in our small bathroom? I don't believe this," Mor moaned.

We both pushed on the door as the horse tried to back out.

"A horse, a horse!" I yelled as Far and Erik came from the living room to help us, and just then the police knocked at our apartment's front door.

They took both Far and Erik to jail and led the racehorse back down to the street, while all the neighbors watched and laughed. Mor was so mad she took the time to scrub the bathroom before bothering to go down to the jailhouse to bail out Far and Erik.

I liked it when Erik and Far were together, because they often included me in what they did. Sometimes they would take me along to outdoor waterfront cafes, and while they drank beer I would play on the fishing boats and feed the ducks. They would also take me with them to see the soccer games. Mor would not go with us because after the game we always ended up back at my Danish grandmother's tavern to eat. Mor did not like to go there much; she didn't like all the drunks and scantily dressed ladies who worked there.

So, I was happy to see that Far was home, and that Erik was with him. When I looked over at him standing next to Far, he gave me a big smile and tossed a box of white Chiclet gum to me. I caught it in my right hand.

Except for Erik, who was smiling as usual, everyone else was in a serious mood. Mor, as she always did when we had company, lit the candles that stood on both sides of the small Danish flag we had on the living room windowsill and then sat down beside Mrs. Johnsen on the couch.

Far picked up his cup to take a sip of coffee and scowled. "Margie, what is wrong with this coffee? It tastes awful!"

"We can't get real coffee beans anymore, only ersatz coffee," Mor said.

"Damn it! First the bakery and now this. Those damn Germans...they are keeping everything for themselves. What's next?" Far grumbled.

"Can't someone fix the static noise from the radio?" said Mrs. Johnsen.

"I will try to tighten the radio tubes," said Erik, as he moved the radio to get to the tubes in the back.

"There, that's better reception...it's clearer now," said Thor.

"What is the radio saying?" I asked, but nobody answered me. I had to listen and try to figure it out for myself. I heard a man saying things like "stay home," "do not go outdoors," and that we were to keep our lights out. He said something about putting up black curtains over our windows, and that we were not ever to go outside after dark.

After that he talked about a man called Hitler. I had heard a lot of people talking about him. One person would say something nice about him to one person, but then they would turn around and say something mean about him to another. It was most puzzling to me. The man on the radio seemed to like him. He talked about how people were trying to poison our minds against him, but we mustn't let them. Then he talked about something called war.

"What is war?" I blurted out. "Is it something bad?"

"Shut up, Johna," Far yelled at me. Mor started talking really fast about Bubbe and Zayde, saying we had to go and get them at once and bring them to our house, but Far interrupted her.

"Stop worrying, Margie. Nothing is going to happen to them here in Denmark," he said.

Then the voice on the radio said something about how all Danes had to surrender all weapons and explosives. Far just laughed.

"No Dane would surrender his arms," he said. "How could the Germans assume that the Danes would be willing to follow such rules, like puppets?"

"Yes, you're right! What kind of bullshit is this?" Erik said.

Far leaned forward, resting his chin on one fist, and listened closely when the announcer said any person who helped the Germans would be protected, but that anyone who tried to hurt those who collaborated against them would be violating the new laws. When the man said the press would be censored by German control and authority, Far shook his head as though he thought they were being silly. But his whole face changed when the radio announcer said that the punishment given by the summary courts for anyone found in possession of a weapon or caught in an act of sabotage would be immediate death.

"Such courts would allow the soldiers to murder Danes," said Far, so angry he almost spit, "just like they did yesterday in Arhus, where they shot a man for treason because he had been caught working with the Danish underground. They can do this and get away with it because not enough Danes are willing to fight back!"

"The Germans have already thrown a number of our leaders into prison. They've also disarmed the Danish Army and put the officers in prison. The police have been left, but who knows for how long?" said Erik.

"Yes," said Far, his eyes narrowed. "I heard they have also replaced the King's royal guards at the gate of the castle. They have even taken some hostages to Horserød Internment Camp."

"Do you have any names of those who were taken there?" asked Thor.

"I don't know," said Far, "they have not released any names."

"What are we to do?" asked Mrs. Johnsen, looking up at the men. "This is all so frightening...rationing our food and closing down our shops for their own use...putting our leaders in jail. And what about Danish Jews?...Are they in danger?" Mrs. Johnsen asked.

"Yes, Poul," said Mor, "what does all this mean?"

"It doesn't mean anything. I tell you, no Danes will be touched. The King stands for that.

The Germans agreed when they occupied us that they would not interfere with the internal affairs of the country. They can't afford to start." Far was confident in his country.

"Much of the world wouldn't agree with you, Poul," said Erik.

"Just tell the all the Jews to stop being Jews," said Far.

"All Jews here are Danes," said Erik. "Every man is a Dane. It doesn't matter whether they are Protestants, Catholics, or Jews. They're Danes, that's all. Of course, they could learn to have more fun," he said, smiling at my mother, "but they're Danes."

"It's naive to believe that the Germans would accept that, and even more naive to believe that they don't desire to imprison all the Jews," said Thor.

"Am I still a Jew?" I whispered to Mrs. Johnson.

"Hush, Johna," was all she said.

"Do not worry yourself," said Far, laughing a little.

"But I've heard rumors that hundreds of Jews have fled Germany," said Erik. He was not usually the serious one. "They are saying that the Germans arrested whole towns at once and loaded them onto trains for work camps. Their only crime was being a Jew, Poul."

"If they lived in Denmark that wouldn't happen," Far said.

"Until today," Thor said. "Until today."

"We've opposed them up to now," said Eric, "with few weapons and only a few people.

Look at the damage the Resistance has done already by blowing up railroad lines and damaging factories. Soon many will be with us," said Erik, looking around at the group.

"Yes," said Thor, nodding his head thoughtfully, "and yesterday they deposed the government. This morning they arrested the entire Danish Army. That shows the Germans are on the run. They must feel they are losing control of the country, which means things could get very dangerous."

Mor and Mrs. Johnsen looked at one another, their faces frozen, and then moved closer to each other on the couch.

"Poul," said Mor, looking at Far. "Are the Jews in danger now in Denmark? Please Poul, get my parents and bring them to our place. They can stay with us until we know it's safe for Jews."

"You have to be kidding! Them living with us?" Far shook his head and snorted, but then he saw tears come into Mor's eyes and softened his tone. "Don't worry, Margie," he said, "I will stop and look in on them to see if they are all right."

Everyone was silent for a moment; they did not seem to know what to say. Erik broke the silence. "It's stupid to believe that the Danes would let the Germans imprison all the Jews."

"We have opposed them up to now," Far said, getting up from his chair and pacing the floor.

"But what was once a clever and bold plan has now become quite dangerous," said Thor.

"Not for all of us, only to those who put themselves in the wrong place at the wrong time," Far replied.

"I don't think so, Poul," said Thor. "I think it is dangerous for everyone now, Dane and Jew alike, even those who have not resisted."

"Hah! Look at my mother's restaurant. Will the soldiers come and close the tavern at curfew? I doubt that will happen," Far shot back.

I listened to all of this as hard as I could. I didn't understand it, but could see how frightened Mor and Mrs. Johnsen were. I looked over at Far. He had something sticking out of his belt. I got up and walked over to him to see what it was. As I reached for he it, he turned and pushed me so hard that I fell on the floor.

"Margie! Do something with her, will you!"

Mor picked me up and took me into the kitchen. Erik followed after us.

"Mor! Mor! Far has a gun," I blurted out.

"Is she all right?" Erik said.

Mor nodded her head. "She will be fine, Erik. Thank you for being so kind. I wish Poul could be more like you."

"Mor, why does far have a gun?" I asked again, plucking at her arm.

"Shush," Mor hissed at me. "Don't tell anyone that Far has a gun. Do you understand?"

"Is it a secret?" I asked.

"Yes, Johna, it's a secret. Do you know how to keep a secret?"

"Oh, yes," I said. This was firm ground for me. "Just ask Far."

"You have secrets with Far?" Mor asked.

"Yes!" I whispered, "but I can't tell you...it's a secret!"

Mor just shook her head at me. "You go back to that footstool and stay put."

I went back into the other room and sat back down on the footstool, staring at their faces as they talked. Even Erik's was serious now.

Chapter 6

Money Coat

After a little while, the radio announcement over, everyone fell silent. Soon Erik, Mrs. Johnsen, and Thor left. Far turned off the radio. He looked over at Mor and nodded his head.

"Put on your coat, Johna," Mor said. " We are going to the store to get black fabric for our windows."

We went down the stairs to the bike shed. The night air was cold and I could see my breath. Far put me on the back seat of his bike, and Mor, in one of her mink coats, was already on hers. For once I was quiet, thinking about what I had heard, wondering what it all meant. At the store, people again stood in long lines—this time lines for just waiting to get into the store. German Gestapo police, who wore black coats and black steel hard hats, stood on either side of the line and shoved us with their rifle butts to keep us in line. Mor tucked me inside her fur coat to warm me.

Peeking out, I suddenly saw Erik and several others running down the street right toward us, with the police chasing after them. When he reached us, he tossed Far something without stopping, and then rushed right on by.

"Here, Johna," Far whispered, shoving two small copper chests at me, "hold these under Mor's coat."

"Poul, there are Germans all around us, please don't do this! Don't get us involved with Erik's shenanigans," Mor begged in a whisper.

"Too late now...so shut your yap, Margit, and act normal. The Nazi watchdogs are perhaps watching us," Far whispered back. After a moment he added, "I heard there was a looting caper at the King's castle. I didn't know Erik was in on it."

"You know too much not to know, Poul," Mor said.

"Mor, these chests are pretty and shiny," I whispered.

"Shh, Johna, hold onto the chests and be quiet. Don't let anybody see them, and don't drop them," Mor said in a stern voice. I could feel Mor shivering as though she were cold. Far got out of the slow line and worked his way to the front, visiting with people all along the way. I saw him slip through the store door ahead of everyone. When he came out, he moved back down the line where we still waited. He took the copper chests from me and stuffed them into the bag he had carried out of the store, covering them with the black cloth he had just bought. We moved slowly out of the line until we reached the corner of Østerbrogade Street. Far looked back to see if anyone were following. No one was, so we got on the bikes again and hurried home.

Erik was waiting for us at the apartment with some boxes piled in front of our doorstep.

"What kept you?" Erik said with a grin.

"I'm here, I'm here. Have you taken leave of your senses, putting us in such an uncomfortable position? You scoundrel," Far said with a laugh.

Mor took the black cloth out of the bag and stomped into the bedroom, yelling, "Get those chests out of my home!"

"I'll take care of it, Margit," Far shouted back.

I stayed in the kitchen with Far and Erik, and watched as they began to put together some clear glass tubing with many twists and turns on iron rod scaffolding. The other boxes Erik had with him had small glass jars and lids in them. When they had put the tubing together, Far lit the gas burner on the stove. I left them and wandered into the bedroom to watch Mor, where she had set up her sewing machine and was doing something with the fabric Far had bought at the store.

"What are you sewing, Mor?" I asked.

"New curtains for our windows," Mor said, without looking up. I turned around and went back into the kitchen. That was more interesting. I sat down in a kitchen chair and watched a liquid boiling in the tubes, with little droplets plunking out the end one drop at the time into one of the small jars.

Far left the kitchen and came back in a moment with towels from the cedar chest. He stuffed them into the gap at the bottom of our kitchen door frame.

"There," he said. "That will help the smell from going into the stairwell."

"It smells like yeast, like Mor making bread," I blurted out.

Far laughed, "Yes, the best kind—Akvavit, good, spiced Danish vodka."

I reached out and put my finger under the spout where the clear liquid dropped into the glass jug. "Ow! It's hot!" I yelled, putting my finger in my mouth to stop the pain.

"Yes, Johna. And let that be a lesson to you to keep your finger out of where it doesn't belong. You just better not tell anyone how you hurt your finger," Far said. "I might get arrested."

"Why do you do it then?" I asked, puzzled.

"Damn it, Johna you do what I say and do not question what I do," Far said. Erik just laughed at us.

"We are bootleggers, Poul, like the Americans," Erik said.

I wandered into the bedroom again to watch Mor sew. "Mor, Far and Erik are making Akvavit schnapps," I said.

"Oy, Johna, get out! Go back to the kitchen!" I didn't move because Mor was not sewing black curtains anymore. Instead she had cut the lining in my blue coat with the brass buttons that Zayde had made for me, and was stuffing paper money inside it. I had seen some strange things in the last few weeks, but this made no sense at all to me.

"Mor, why are you putting money in my coat?"

Mor grabbed both my arms and said, "Johna, I know you can't understand any of this, but the German soldiers you see are bad and will steal our money, so we must hide it."

"Is all stealing bad?" I thought of the Germans that day when they took Laurel and Hardy's grapes, when Peter took the apple, and then I thought of Mor's mink coats and the pretty copper chests. "Is Erik bad?"

"Johna," she said, her eyes narrow, her mouth hard.

"Mor," I whined, "don't be mad at me!"

"Hush," she said. "I'm not mad. Erik is good and the Germans are bad. That's all your need to know."

"But Zayde says stealing is a bad thing.

"Shush, we aren't going to talk about this. You'll understand when you grow up."

"Is this a secret, too?"

"Oy," said Mor. "Yes, it's a secret."

"Are we hiding the copper chests from the Germans?"

"Yes. Just trust me and your father, but no one else. You mustn't tell anyone, not even Hanne, about this money in your coat. It's a secret for you to keep—a very big secret—and you are big girl. Don't tell anyone. Do you hear me?"

"Yes, Mor."

"You won't even know it's there. Now stop asking questions."

Suddenly I had so many secrets, filling me up like too many bagels. I went back to the kitchen again. Far and Erik were putting the tiny jars full of Akvavit into small boxes, and when they finished they hurried out the front door saying they were going to sell the alcohol to Erik's friends. Mor and I cleaned up the kitchen.

When we were done we headed into the living room. Mor sat down on the sofa and leaned back with her eyes closed.

"Can you read the ugly duckling story to me?" I asked Mor.

"All right, Johna. Come here with me," she said, patting the sofa next to her. I sat down beside her. She hadn't read long before we were asleep in each other's arms.

Keeping secrets was tiring work for both of us.

Chapter 7

Unwelcome Attention

On Thursday that same week, Hanne and I were headed down the street to school. We chatted about getting together after school to trade more napkins. In spite of all the unusual things that had been happening in our world, some threads of our normal lives continued on. Valby Elementary School was a large gray building covered with green ivy. An imaginary line divided the school in half, one side for girls, one for boys. Each schoolroom had high ceilings and wide, dark, wood trim. In addition, each one had a picture of King Christian X on the wall, along with pictures of the town square and the Parliament building.

I hurried up the unpainted wooden steps to the back of our classroom and hung my wool sweater on the hook with the other coats. Since Mor had stuffed money into my blue police coat, she did not want me to wear it to school. If I did not have it on, I would not be tempted to tell its secret.

When we were settled behind our desks, our teacher, Sven Oldstrom, entered the room. We all stood up next to our seats to greet him. Mr. Oldstrom was Swedish, and like many others of his countrymen, had come to Denmark to work.

"Good morning," he said in a soft, gentle voice. "You may all sit back down in your seats now. Today we are going to learn the legend of Beowoulf, a tale about Danes in ancient times and their troubles with a monster of the deep. The myth tells how the hero Beowoulf died destroying a gigantic evil creature named Grendel, and freed his village from harm. Because he was so brave, the Danish King buried Beowoulf with all his treasures."

"Why was he so brave?" I asked.

"Children, some people are more brave than others because they have something special inside them that makes them fearless and brave...it's like a special magic."

"My father is brave and so am I, and I can keep secrets," I blurted out.

"Quiet, Johna, and turn around in your seat," Mr. Old-strom said. I could hear the snickering of the other kids. Embarrassed, I put on one of my best frowns and crossed my arms across my chest. I kept quiet for the rest of the lesson as Mr. Old-strom told us the story of how Beowoulf fought the evil demon Grendel. Soon it was time for our morning break.

"It is now time for recess, so go, be orderly, and put on your coats," said Mr. Oldstrom.

I ran to our coat racks in the back of the room.

"Where is your blue coat, Johna?" asked Mr. Oldstrom when he saw me putting on my wool sweater.

"Someone stole it," I said without thinking. "I can't find it."

"We will have to check the lost and found locker," Mr. Old-strom said.

"You had it on yesterday, when I saw you go to the store with your mor," Hanne said.

"I hate that blue coat anyway," I said too loudly, confused about the predicament I was in and glad Zayde couldn't hear me. Mr. Oldstrom just shook his head, and hurried us out to the playground.

The boys were playing kickball. Hanne, Else, and I went to the play box and pulled out three jump ropes. I would hold one end of the rope in the crook of my left arm, the other in my right hand, and could skip rope as well as anyone. We started to play a game of who could skip rope the longest before tripping up.

Suddenly Peter and two other boys moved up in front of me, leering, and blocking my rope.

"Anybody a Jew here?" Peter yelled.

"You are a Jew, aren't you, Johna?" another boy said.

"None of your business," I answered as we stopped skipping ropes. Peter and the boys moved closer to me.

"Hey, little Jew," said Peter. "Jews were Christ killers, that makes you a killer, too—a blind, crippled, one-armed, stupid Jew." He mocked me as the other boys surrounded me. Peter stepped closer to me and spit on my glasses. Hanne and the other girls backed away until I stood alone, alone and scared. My nose started to run and I felt tears forming.

"Leave me alone!" I yelled, wanting to fit in, knowing I couldn't.

"Oh, the Jew can talk! Who will stop me from chasing you out of this school yard?" asked Peter, his face twisted into a sneer.

"I will, young man," said Mr. Oldstrom, stepping up from behind them. "You boys, meet me in the headmaster's office right now. Go!"

I wanted to be brave like Beowoulf. I wanted so much to blacken Peter's eye and hurt him, just as Beowoulf had hurt the monster that threatened him. But I couldn't. Instead, Mrs. Hansen, Hanne's mother, took me to the teachers' coffee room and left me there. I sat there and waited, not knowing what else to do. After a while, the door opened and Mor came in. She had a funny look on her face and sat beside me.

"I heard what happened this morning," she said, and gave me a hug, holding me tight.

"I'm taking you out of school early today. You can go to the market with me...how will that be?" she asked, and squeezed me again.

I nodded, suddenly feeling like I wanted to cry. I didn't know why Peter had said the things he had, didn't even know what he meant by most of those things. It was true I was a Jew, and it was true I only had one arm, but these things weren't new and I couldn't see why they mattered to him. I only knew he had wanted to hurt me for some reason. But I thought of Far telling me I had to be brave girl and not cry, and held back my tears.

Mor and I left the schoolhouse. When we reached where she had left her bicycle, she put me on the seat rack behind her and then pedaled away to the Gammelstrand, an open fish market near the water. Once there, all the many sights, sounds, and smells took over my attention and I quickly forgot about the things Peter had said. Seagulls swarmed overhead begging for scraps of fish, and soon I was laughing at their play as they fought over any fish they could steal. Women wearing white kerchiefs on their heads and long, dirty aprons stood in the many stalls and yelled out to the crowd, "Fresh fish just caught! Get your fresh fish here!" Everywhere I looked I saw piles of fish and shellfish or nets, floats, and rigging.

Mor bought some codfish from one of the yelling women, and then we started to walk back to the light pole where we had left her bike. A German officer approached us and knelt down to get at my eye level.

"Hello, little girl...you want this chocolate bar?" he said, handing me the candy. I could only stare at him in surprise, so the soldier opened my right hand, then closed my fist around the chocolate bar.

"Be a good girl for your pretty mother," he said walking away, smiling.

I stared at the chocolate bar, unable to believe my good luck from a bad German, but Mor quickly took it from me and dropped it on the ground in front of us.

"Mor, no!" I said, not wanting to lose so precious a thing as a chocolate bar. "That's chocolate!" But my complaining did no good. She picked me up and sat me down with a hard thump on the back of her bike seat. Before I could say anything more, Neils Strum, the policeman who lived downstairs from us, skidded his bicycle to a stop in front of us.

"Margit," he said, touching her arm, "it is better that you don't take these trips. The fish workers sometimes turn in Jews to the Germans."

Mor just looked at him. Then, without saying a word, she put the fish package in the bike basket and pedaled for home. Twice now in the same morning it was somehow bad to be Jewish.

That evening as we were sitting down to dinner, Mor told Far what had happened at school and the fish market that day. He frowned and shook his head.

"Johna is not to go to school anymore, and that is final," Far said, scooping me onto his lap. "And you," he said to me, "you are not to talk about Jewish things anymore. You're a Danish little girl. Can you remember that, Johna?"

"But, Far," I said. He raised his hand to stop me from finishing my sentence. "Not a Jew! You're not a Jew," he said again. I looked over at Mor, and she nodded her head.

"Is it another secret?" I asked.

"Yes, Little Skat. Now go get me a beer," Far said as he patted my behind. I jumped down from his lap to get his beer.

How does one forget secrets and such a thing as being Jewish? I wondered.

Chapter 8

Air Raids

Later that night sirens wailing in the night scared me awake. Mor and Far certainly had known this was coming, and had prepared for it by keeping clothes near the bed. But I didn't know what any of that talk meant. All I knew was I had never heard a such a noise in all my life and I was terrified. I didn't know what was happening and opened my eyes to see Far standing at the end of my bed yelling at me to get up.

"Johna! Let's go!" I could see him putting his trousers on.

"Hurry!" said Mor. "Get on all the clothes that I put on the end of your bed. Now!" Mor jerked the comforter off me and rushed about the bedroom, finding her own clothing, and Far's.

"It's closer," Mor said as the noise of shooting and explosions increased.

I climbed out of my bed to put on all the clothes Mor had hung on the end of my bed: three pair of underwear, two pair of socks, and two shirts, all to be worn under my regular clothes. On top of that, she had told me, I was to put on my blue "money" coat.

Just then someone banged on our apartment door.

"To the shelters, hurry!" yelled a man whose voice I did not recognize.

All the noise hurt my ears and made me afraid. I tried to hurry and dress, but it was hard. I couldn't make my arms work right. My feet kept going in the wrong holes of my underpants, my head couldn't find the neck of my shirts. Mor, finished with her own dressing, came over to me get into all my clothes and then into my coat. When I had everything on, I felt so fat I could hardly move.

"Here, Johna," she said, "take this paper. I'll bring crayons so you can draw while we are in the shelter."

I was just reaching for it when I heard several loud cracks outside. Mor looked up.

"Gunfire!" she cried, freezing where she stood. She looked at Far, "It's getting closer, Poul!"

"Margit!" Far snapped at her, "keep moving here!"

She turned toward him, her eyes wide.

"Don't worry," said Far. "Those guns are ours. It's the Krauts who need to worry. There was a riot today in the shipyard. Men refused to repair the German ships and soldiers attacked them. Tonight Germany pays. We're sinking ships and taking revenge."

Far scooped me up and we all three ran to the stairs. As we hurried down, I heard lots of other footsteps pounding down the winding stairwell. Everybody in the building was running down the stairs.

"Poul," said Mor between breaths, "how do you know this?"

"How do you think I know? Where do you think I go?" he whispered back to her. "Those damn Nazis think they're perfect, the perfect race. Well, they're perfect asses."

"Poul, please," said Mor.

"They weren't so perfect when the coffee train blew up," he continued. Far was furious, talking more to himself than to Mor. "They're not going to use Danish trains to steal our meat and coffee. Not without a price. And they're not going to be allowed to lock up Danish Jews." When we got outside, the siren blared so loudly that it made my whole body vibrate. I buried my face in Far's coat to block the noise. In only a few more moments, though, we were down the stairs into the coal cellar.

"What? What are you saying? Are they planning to do that?" Mor asked "What about your German friends...couldn't they protect us?"

Far set me down in the hallway and we walked down a long dark passage until we came to the coal cellar that was now our air raid shelter. "No German will protect you. None. Only I can protect you and Johna."

"But they're soldiers! They have guns," said Mor. "Won't they help you?"

"Margit, wake up," said Far, losing patience. "The Germans may not stand for Jews to remain here much longer."

"But you said they wouldn't dare take Danish Jews!"

"They can, and they will," said Far. "Remember what Thor said last week? Well, he was right. And every time you go to your father's house you put yourself and Johna in danger. Every time.

Now that they've stolen the lists, it's only a matter of time before they start rounding people up here just like they have elsewhere."

Mor clung to Far's arm, stumbling along beside him in the dark corridor. "What are we to do?" she said. "What about Zayde and Bubbe?"

"Just calm down, Margit. I will think of something," said Far.

We came to the end of the hallway and entered what used to be the coal cellar for our apartment building. It was a large room ringed by little cells with black bars on them for holding in the coal. Though we no longer used to coal to heat with, the cement floor still had a layer of black soot. The only light in the room was a single bare bulb that hung from the ceiling. It hurt my eyes to look at it.

I looked around the strange room and saw our neighbors were all there, sitting on wooden benches at a long wooden table. I knew Far had built the table with wood he had brought home from work. It was fresh, new wood, and reminded me of my doll house that Far had built for me. It was a small feeling of familiarity.

Hanne was already sitting at the table, holding her red umbrella. I went over and squeezed in beside her. We just sat there, quiet, unsure, and listened to the grown-ups talk around us.

"That bombing sounds close," said one woman.

"One of these days, they'll hit our building," said another.

"The building would fall and crush us all in here!" said the first woman.

Hanne and I looked at one another. Much had happened that I didn't understand, but a building falling on me was something I could imagine and I wanted to leave.

"What if the building falls on us, Hanne? I whispered. "I'm afraid!"

"I'm not a bit afraid," she said, but her eyes were wide and dark, and I knew she was lying.

"You're not?" I asked, but before she could answer, I could hear what sounded like fireworks outside. "Listen, Hanne!" I said. "It sounds like someone is setting off fireworks. I wish I were outside so I could watch, don't you?"

Hanne didn't answer me and I didn't say anything more. The air in the cellar was damp and chilly, and smelled like mildew. Many of the adults smoked pipes, cigars, and cigarettes, filling the air with smoke that stung my eyes and made them water.

"Mor, can we draw with our crayons on the wall?" I asked, anxious for something to do. By way of an answer, Mor pulled the crayons she'd brought for me out of her pocket and handed them to me. I gave some to Hanne and we each set about drawing our own picture. Hanne drew a girl with a red umbrella just like the one she had. I drew a stick man with a Jewish cap on his head. Hanne looked over at my little man, and then suddenly, she threw the crayons at me.

"Why did you do that!?" I said, surprised and hurt, but she turned away from me and wouldn't answer. Trying to think of something to say, something that turned everything back to normal, I asked, "Hanne, may I see your umbrella?"

"No!" Hanne yelled, and stuck her tongue out at me. "My mother says that I cannot play with you anymore."

It was as if she had kicked me. Hanne, my best friend—Hanne, with whom I shared everything—was telling me suddenly she couldn't play with me anymore. After all that had happened that day, I got so upset that I screamed and lunged at her with my left arm. It fit right into her eye socket, blackening her eye in an instant.

"Johna!" said Mor. "I'm ashamed of you, what makes you have such a temper to hit Hanne? Far will deal with you when we get home."

"She said I'm not her friend anymore," I whimpered, looking at Far across the table. To my surprise, he gave me a smile, and then winked at me. I tugged on Mor's coat, "Look, Mor, Far is not mad at me," I said.

"Be quiet, Johna," said Mor, looking around at the others who were all watching. "We don't hit other people."

Outside, the shooting grew even louder.

"The firing is close," the landlord said.

"Don't worry," said Far. "The Danish underground is getting a little revenge for all the stealing the Germans have been doing."

"So Poul, this does not worry you? If you know so much

perhaps this is just a false alarm and we should go back to our beds," the landlord replied. "How do you know this information?"

"I find out things," said Far, rising from the table. "I find out things." Without another word, he left the coal cellar and went back out into the night.

"Where's Far going?" I asked Mor.

Mor's eyes followed Far as he went through the door. She didn't answer me, but pulled me close to her. The neighbors stared at us, their eyes dark in the glare of the light bulb. I slid off the bench and hid under the table. I sat there, leaning against Mor's legs and looked at a magazine that had fallen there until the sound of the sirens changed. I heard a short blast, followed by a very low sound. Then Mor ducked her head under the table.

"That means we can go home now, Johna. Go get your crayons and paper."

Everyone around us began to get up and move around. People had brought food and drink with them and Mor helped to clean up the table. I tried to see where Hanne was, but she had already gone. She had not said good-bye to me.

When we finally climbed back up to our apartment, Far came in the door just behind us. He was all wet, had obviously been out in the rain.

Mor quickly peeled all my clothes off me and hung them on the bed rail until the next time the sirens sounded. I lay there for a little bit, unable to sleep. So much had happened to me in the last few days, so many things that hurt or puzzled. And now even by best friend had said we were not friends anymore. Far had said I wasn't to go to school anymore. What had happened? How had it changed, I wondered. In the other room, Mor and Far stayed up in the night talking.

Chapter 9

Jews Must Hide

All the next week I had to stay in our apartment most of the time. As Far had said, I no longer went to school. I thought I would like that at first, but I soon grew lonely and missed not seeing my friends. None of them came to our house. I missed Hanne, and was sadder than I had ever been before. I know it was hard on Mor, too.

When I woke on Friday of that week, I peeked out from under the blackout curtains and watched the sun coming through the gray clouds. Mor and Far were already up and getting dressed.

"It's almost Rosh Hashanah, Poul, and I promised my parents to be with them for the special service," Mor said.

"If I say you can't go, you will go anyway, so I will tag along with you. I'll even fetch Erik and have him drive us," Far said.

"I'm glad you care enough to protect us," said Mor.

"Why wouldn't I?" said Far, and with that, he picked up his coat and left to find Erik.

I got up, got dressed, and then Mor and I waited for Far to come back. I was happy to be going out at last. I was also excited that Erik would be coming with us, and couldn't help wondering if perhaps he would have something for me, as he always did.

"Should I wear my blue coat, Mor?" I asked. I had already grabbed my doll, Jette.

"Yes, it makes Zayde happy to see you wearing it, but no telling of the money in your coat, Johna!"

"*Ja*, Mor, it will be our secret."

Soon Far came up the stairs.

"Let's go. Erik will be here in a few minutes," said Far, all business.

Once outside we waited in the sunlight for Erik. It was late September, but the sun still had a bit of warmth to it when it came out from behind the clouds, and it felt good to feel it on my face. In only a minute or so, Erik's car came gliding around the corner and rolled to a stop in front of us. We all climbed in.

Riding in a car was always a special treat for me, for it did not happen often in those days.

After we were settled in the back seat of Erik's car, he tossed some coins at me, and grinned at me in the rear-view mirror. I smiled back and waved at him. As always, he had remembered me.

In moments, we were on our way. The engine shook and roared like a lion as we charged through the back streets of Copenhagen. Soon we pulled up to the curb in front of Zayde and Bubbe's apartment. Suddenly I was happy to be going to see them, my earlier sadness forgotten.

We climbed the stairs to their apartment, and while we waited in front of Zayde and Bubbe's door, Far smirked and started to laugh at the small box on the doorframe.

"I see his little box, or what ever he calls it, is at an angle again, even after I straightened it for him the last time I was here," he said, pointing to Zayde's mezuzah.

"Why do you continue to annoy my father? You know perfectly well the mezuzah is hung at an angle on purpose," said Mor, reaching out to block Far from touching the box.

"Zayde told me that the small wooden case on the doorframe contains a scroll with words from the Bible to keep evil and bad things away," I said. "Perhaps that means the Germans!"

Far just glared at me as Mor knocked on the door. When we entered, Zayde waved his hand toward Far. Far nodded and said, "Good day, to you." Then he handed Zayde a cigar.

"Thanks, Poul...how's work?"

"Fine," said Far. "A job is a job."

Bubbe came over to me and gave me a hug. Then she handed out cookies to all of us.

"Papa is almost out of cigars, Poul," said Mor. "Why don't you and Johna go down to Isaac's cigar store to buy him some? It will give me time to clean and dust this place before we go to synagogue." It was hard for Bubbe to clean properly any more, since she could hardly see, so Mor always did some cleaning whenever she could.

"You go ahead and clean for your mother, and we will be back soon," Far said, and he and I left for town.

Far and I walked to Strøget, the strolling street. This little street was lined with antique and souvenir shops, clothing stores, and bars. Outdoor restaurants, as well as tobacco, fruit, and flower stands filled the sidewalks. Boys selling newspapers wandered amongst the shoppers. The whole street was an exciting place to me, with all its business and activity, but my most favorite places of all were the hot dog and ice cream vendors' stalls. I had high hopes of interesting Far in one of these, too.

We headed down the sidewalk toward the cigar store. As we came to a small curve in the street, we came upon three German soldiers standing under the two flagpoles that marked the front of Isaac's cigar store. A flag with the German swastika flew from one flagpole. The red and white flag of Denmark still fluttered in the wind on the other pole, but the soldiers were starting to take this one down, too. I could hear Isaac yelling at the German soldiers.

"Why is the German soldier trying to take down the Danish flag?" I said, tilting my head for a better view. "It doesn't look like Denmark anymore without our flag."

"Shut up, Johna. Stay here and don't move till I get back!" Far left me where I was and strolled up to the storefront.

"What's wrong, Old Isaac?" Far asked.

Isaac blurted out to Far, "Why can't they leave at least the one Danish flag up? We always fly Danish flags! Is this not still Denmark?"

One of the soldiers drew his pistol and pointed it at Far while the other soldier lowered the Danish flag and replaced it with another German swastika flag.

"*Ja, Ja,*" Far said, raising his hands up.

"Go away, Christensen," Isaac said suddenly to Far. "I don't need your help."

The soldier holding the gun shouted, "Go! This is none of your business!" Far backed away slowly until he reached a certain distance. Then he stood very still. The soldier waved his gun at him again. "Walk away, or we will arrest you!"

Far moved away then. Just as he came back to me, a small truck with a tarp-covered back arrived in front of the cigar store. Inside were two more German soldiers. While we watched, they climbed down, grabbed Isaac, and shoved him in the back of the truck. One of the soldiers banged his fist on the side, and the truck drove off. Another soldier nailed a board across the cigar shop and wrote "JUDEN" (JEWS) in chalk on the board. Far grabbed my hand and we hurried back to Zayde's.

"Where are they taking Isaac?" I asked.

"Never mind, Johna. And don't tell Mor—or Zayde and Bubbe—what we saw...about old Isaac being taken away in the truck. All right? The Germans just want to talk to him. We don't want to worry Mor, do we?"

"Is this another secret between you and me, Far?"

"Yes, yes, it's another secret." Far was silent a moment, then suddenly he struck his fist into his other open hand and swore. He turned his collar up on his coat, and adjusted his hat lower on his forehead. Then he looked down at me and smiled.

"Here, Johna," he said, "here's some money for your piggy bank, OK?"

It was hard enough to understand about the soldier pointing a gun at Far, but I didn't know what to think about Isaac being taken away in that truck. How could I not say something to Mor? She would want to know why we didn't bring back any cigars. This was almost too much of a secret for me to keep.

When we came back to the apartment, we found Mor was alone, dusting the furniture.

"You're already back?" Mor said to Far as she dusted the sewing table.

"Where are your parents?" he asked in response.

"Taking a walk, why? Did you get some cigars for Papa?"

"No, the shop's closed," said Far, and gave me a cold glare to remind me to keep our secrets.

"Why would it be closed?"

"I don't know, Margit," Far said with impatience. "Listen, I have to leave. Erik and I will pick you and Johna up at seven tonight after the synagogue service." With that, Far opened the door again and left.

I began to help Mor dust and to my relief she didn't ask me anything more about the cigar store. When Zayde and Bubbe returned from their stroll, we ate some apple slices dipped in honey, and then left for the synagogue.

Once inside the synagogue, we climbed the familiar stairs to the balcony and Zayde went to his place on the main floor. The service started with the usual blast from the twisted horn. (Shofar). I settled in between Mor and Bubbe. We could hear the loud murmurs of men's voices below us. I leaned over the balcony railing to get a better view. Rabbi Melchior, however, stopped the service before it even got started.

"Everyone, please listen! There will be no service today!" he yelled out. "I have just received word that the Germans are planning to round up all Jews in Denmark tomorrow and ship them to work camps." People began shouting and all talking at once in a panic, their voices echoing off the walls of the great hall.

"Please!" the rabbi continued, his voice shaking, "This synagogue is now closed. The Germans will be coming for you at your homes tomorrow, so you must all leave your homes immediately and hide. Just gather up what you need, your small valuables, and hide with friends. Then, just wait. Many people are trying to help and we will find ways to safety. When we do, we will then come and find you. We must warn everyone. Now, go! Go quickly, and may God be with you!"

The three of us left the balcony, struggling to follow the other women down the stairs to the crowded synagogue foyer. My skin prickled. Go and hide from the Germans?! What did that mean? People all around me were talking loud, pushing, some women had begun to cry. I grew so afraid, and shied away from everyone until Mor grabbed my hand. Finally, Zayde found us and we left for their apartment.

"This is unholy, interrupting a service," Zayde blurted out. Then he turned to Bubbe and in a voice almost like a child's said, "Where will we go? Malka and Johna are Jews, too. Must we all hide?"

"Am I a Jew again, Mor?" I asked, unable to keep track of my rapidly shifting status.

"What else does my Johna have to bear? No hand, bad eyesight, and now she can't be a little Jew," Mor blurted out. Then she stopped short, and turning to me, said." No, Johna! We are not Jews. We are Danes, remember? Now be quiet!"

"*Oy, gervaldt!*" Zayde said, and banged his Bible hard on the table.

"I'm sorry, Papa, I'm just upset," Mor said. "Please understand why I say this!"

I hugged my doll close to me and wondered who I was.

"Papa, you will come and live with us. We will wait for Poul to come," Mor said. "You'll be safe there, you'll see!"

"Why do they have to hide?" I asked, but no one answered me.

Zayde just stood staring at nothing, his face dark. Mor began to help Bubbe pack their old suitcases. When they had put everything in they could fit, they sat down and we all waited for Far to return.

A little while later, Far burst through the door.

"What the hell is going on?" asked Far, pointing his finger at the people milling outside in the hallway of the senior apartment hall.

"Do not swear in my house, Poul," was all the answer Zayde gave.

Mor told Far what had happened at the synagogue service. "The Rabbi said the Jews are being rounded up, that we must all hide," she said.

"I'm being carted away like a piece of luggage," said Zayde, talking to no one in particular. "I'm tired and old. This is not happiness in my life now, to run." He turned to Far. "If there is anything of decency left in you, Poul, please leave my wife and me alone. You are an intruder in my home. Now leave!" Zayde waved a hand toward the door, but it had no strength in it.

"You don't need to be rude, though I see your Danish improves quite a bit when you have something to say. I also see that in years you are an old man, but there must be something in you yet that is still young, something that still wants to live," said Far.

"I just dream of going to Palestine one day, Poul. Why would a poor simple Jew like me want to run?" Zayde sat down at the table, putting both his hands in front of him, staring at them as though they belonged to someone else.

"We are talking about lives, human beings, not Jews," Mor said.

"I am frightened. I'm terribly frightened," said Bubbe, looking at Zayde.

"Please, Papa, you have no choice." Mor moved closer to Zayde.

"Come, we'll all go to our apartment and figure this out," Far said, and beckoned Zayde to come with him. Zayde closed his eyes tight for a moment, and then with his head down, he lifted himself from the table.

Far had found Erik again and all six of us crammed into his black car. As we drove along the streets, we could see German soldiers patrolling with police dogs on strong leather leashes. We turned down one street and saw some more of them kicking a man who was lying in the gutter. I had never seen such a thing and hid my eyes with my hand.

"Why are they doing that and being so mean?" I asked.

"Because they *are* mean!" Zayde answered.

When we got home, Erik and Far carried the suitcases into the living room. Zayde sat in Far's chair.

"My violin! Where is my violin?" Zayde said, as his eyes searched amongst the two pieces of luggage on the floor.

"I brought it. It's right here," Bubbe reassured him, pointing at the violin case.

Then Far took a silver flask from his back pocket and offered it to Zayde, who drank from it and handed it back to Far.

"Gut, sehr gut," Zayde nodded, and wiped his lips with his hand.

"Listen to me," Far said. "I suggest strongly that you shave off your beard—that would be safer for you—you won't look so much like a Jew then. Erik and I will find a place for you to hide. Meanwhile, stay put here until I can find out what is really going on. I'll return as soon as I can."

"Take Johna with you, Poul. It's too much for her to see her grandparents upset and afraid," said Mor.

Erik grinned at me and took my hand. The three of us left the apartment and Erik drove us to the Absalon Tavern, my Danish grandmother's tavern.

My Danish grandmother's name was Poulene, but I called her Farmor, which was Danish for "father's mother." She was a big woman, round with fat. She had big blue eyes, and wore her tight, dark brown curls cropped short. She was my grandmother, but she was not at all like Bubbe, who made cookies and gave me candy. Farmor smoked cigars, and used swear words just like Far did.

Her tavern served liquor, as well as other things. Small rooms lined the second floor of the tavern and Farmor would tell the ladies who were in them which customers they should drink with. To a seven-year-old, this was just the way things were done. It was years before I realized my farmor ran a tavern *and* a brothel.

Olof, my Danish grandfather, could not work in the tavern anymore, as his hands would shake and tremble too badly to serve drinks. He lived alone down by the harbor, but he would still come to the tavern and drink—Farmor said that was the one place his hands were steady, when they held his own beer.

We parked the car and then went around to the back of the tavern. As we came in the back door to the kitchen, we could see Farmor talking to the cooks. Far crossed over to her and with a touch, drew her back toward the door where Erik and I were standing.

"Alfred is in the tavern," he whispered. "His motorcycle is parked out front. You know him—he's the German that I met when I used to attend the Nazi meetings. We're still friends, and as I told you, he is going with Emma that Jewish girl who comes here with him once in a while. He said he wants to help with the Jewish situation. Ask him to come upstairs. I need to talk to him."

"Are you sure you can trust being around him?" asked Farmor.

"Just go get him!" Far whispered back at her.

We left the kitchen and climbed up the back stairs to one of the empty girls' rooms. We closed the door and sat on the bed to wait in silence.

Someone knocked at the door. Far got up to open it and Farmor came in, followed by two German soldiers. She closed the door and leaned against it. Far stood up and shook hands with Alfred, while I hid behind Erik. Germans were bad. Germans stole fruit, took away cigar store owners, and kicked people. But they also gave out chocolate, and now, here was Far, going to Germans to get help for Zayde and Bubbe. How was one supposed to know when they were bad and when they were good?

"Who's that with you?" Far asked Alfred.

"This is Carl," said Alfred, motioning toward the man with him. "He can be trusted."

"I need some information, Alfred. We must talk," Far said.

Alfred was tall with big blue eyes and a small nose. He had shiny, straight blond hair. The other German, Carl, had narrow hazel eyes and his blond hair was curly. In uniform they looked like twin toy soldiers.

"I have wanted to talk to you, too. The lady, Emma, you introduced to me at the nightclub a few months ago? I love her, but I'm pissed off at you! Did you know she was Jewish when you introduced us?" Alfred said.

"No, Alfred. Honest, I didn't know," said Far.

"What a mess I'm in! But right now I want to help Emma hide so we can be together when this war is all over." Alfred took his long cigarette holder out of his mouth, removed the butt and dropped it on the floor, grinding it under his heel. Farmor glared at him, but clenched her teeth and said nothing.

Carl peeked behind Erik at me. I stared at him and moved closer to the other side of Erik.

"What happen to her left hand? Let me see it," said Carl, and moved toward me.

"No!" I said. I shivered and wondered if Far could see my fear. I worried that I was not being brave as he expected me to be. I covered my head under Erik's jacket. Farmor came over and sat next to Erik to help hide me from Carl.

"Her hand was an accident," Far said, moving to stand in front of me, too.

"Forget it, Carl" Alfred said.

"It embarrasses her. Don't be mean," said Alfred, and waved Carl away. "Back off, I say, you are scaring the little girl."

Carl laughed and backed away.

"You know, Poul, unfortunately, you can never be sure whom you can trust. But you and I must come to an agreement and keep this meeting a secret. From all accounts, Hitler's in a rage, blaming the Danish Jews for all the sabotage that's been happening lately—for blowing up the railroad tracks and train cars so that they can't transport food to Germany, and for destroying some of the ships in the harbor. He has issued a final order that all the Jews must be rounded up and deported to work camps."

"Well, it isn't just Jews," Farmor said. "I know six Danes who were sentenced to thirty days for insulting German officers."

"That is so true," Carl said with a grin.

"That's nuts!" Far exploded. "That's the kind of thinking that made me stop going to those Nazi meetings." Then just as quickly he stopped himself, then he laughed. "Next thing we know," he said in a jovial way, "they'll be arresting Danes who are married to Jews!"

"Some Danes involved with Jews have already been arrested, Poul," Alfred said.

"No, how can that be? Have I been misled?" Far closed his right hand over his left and squeezed his knuckles until they popped.

"Listen, Poul, I don't want to hear anymore. I don't care what we Germans do and how many people we have to arrest. Let's just you and I work together to help Emma and your family...agreed?"

"Yes, of course, Alfred," Far said, his face empty of all expression.

"God damn it, I'm a soldier, Poul! But I do not choose to hurt innocent human beings. I am a German, a trusted officer, and I could get shot for treason for doing this! Even just having this meeting is dangerous for me!" Alfred began to pace the floor.

Carl eyes followed him back and forth. "Perhaps we should not get so involved with helping Poul's family," he said. "These are dangerous times."

"These are not normal times, Carl. I need him to help Emma, and Poul is willing to help his wife's family and needs help with that. Understand?" Carl didn't say anything back but just looked at Alfred.

Far turned to Alfred. "Do you know a hiding place for my wife's parents?"

For a few moments it was silent in the room, and I shifted slightly, to see what was happening. I saw Far take out his pipe, put it in his mouth, and hold it tight in his teeth while he looked firmly at Alfred. As Far groped in his pocket for matches, I could see his hands were trembling. He pressed in the imitation tobacco with his thumb and struck the match under his shoe, all without taking his eyes off of Alfred. I peeked from behind Erik's jacket as the smoke curled upward, between the two men.

"All right, Poul," said Alfred at last, looking hard into Far's face. "I will give you an address and a key to a house that a family has already vacated. It will not be searched again. I'll make sure of that." He pulled out a piece of paper and a pencil from his pocket and wrote out something on it. From another pocket, he fished out a set of keys. He handed both the paper and the keys to Far. "All right?"

Far nodded his head once.

"Now you have to do your part of the bargain," said Alfred. Then, without another word, the two Germans turned and left the room, walking in long strides to the metallic click of their leather boots on the floor. I stayed hidden behind Eric and Farmor until I heard them go down the wooden stairs to the tavern.

Chapter 10

The White Brigade

After the meeting with Alfred and Carl ended, Far, Erik, and I left to go back to our apartment. When we arrived home, Zayde, Bubbe, and Mor were still in the living room waiting our return.

"Poul, I have seen Germans roaming the neighborhood. What are we to do?" Mor asked.

"Things are getting worse. Your parents can't stay here. Your rabbi was right, the Germans are rounding up the Jews, but Erik and I found a place for your parents to hide. There is a house in Gilleleje a couple of miles away on the outskirts of Copenhagen. No one will suspect,"

Far said, as he bent down in front of Zayde. "I told you that your beard is a danger. It is a dead giveaway that you are a Jew. You must cut it off! Now!"

Mor repeated Far's words, but Zayde turned away from Far and remained silent.

"You can use my razor or anything else you need to shave," said Far.

"Thank you, but I don't shave," said Zayde, still not looking at him.

"What do you mean?"

"I cannot use a razor."

"What the hell's the matter? Why not?"

"I am not allowed to use that sort of thing. Moses has directed that we must only cut it, not shave it," Zayde said.

"Damn it, Margit!" said Far, turning to Mor in exasperation. "Tell him I have a gadget that merely cuts the beard. Now tell him to go do it! He's putting you all in danger with his stupid beliefs." Far shook his head.

"Come, I will help you," said Bubbe, motioning to Zayde.

I ran to Mor and straddled her lap. She folded her arms around me and held me close, pressing her face into my hair.

"Far was talking to some Germans soldiers at Farmor's," I

whispered to Mor. Mor turned to Far. "Come here, Poul. You are involved with some Germans?"

"What?!...No, I'm not involved, only trying to do the right thing and to help the best I can. Why don't you trust me?"

"Johna says she saw you talking to German soldiers. A whole part of your life is a secret to me. Do you know that? What am I supposed to think about that? What are you doing?"

"I am doing things to help, Margit. That's the truth."

Erik, with his dashing smile, came over and gave Mor a kiss on the cheek. "Do not worry, Margit."

"Hah! Not worry you say. Why should I listen to you, a man who never did an honest day's work!" Mor pushed him away.

After a little while Zayde came back to the living room. His face looked white with his beard gone. He looked like a stranger to me. I whispered to Mor, "I don't like Zayde's looks without his beard."

"Margit, tell your father to try to get some sun or makeup on his face so he doesn't look so pale," Far said. "Now let's go. We need to be on our way."

We all left in Erik's car. I was crammed in the back seat with Mor, Bubbe, and Zayde. Far and Erik sat in the front seat. Far leaned forward and tapped his pipe on the ashtray. We were all silent except Bubbe, who kept murmuring prayers and kissing me on the forehead. There was too much praying, too much kissing, too much silence, and too much of everything.

We drove out of Copenhagen and into the countryside. Finally, the car stopped in front of a house in the fishing village of Gilleleje.

"Looks like this is it," said Erik.

We all got out and climbed a short flight of stone steps. Far unlocked the glass entryway.

The house had the feeling that someone still lived there, with polished furniture, music boxes, and red, white, yellow, and green watercolor paintings on the walls. All around on the table tops were scattered family pictures of people I didn't know. Soup bowls on the kitchen table still held the cold remains of someone's dinner.

"Poul, where are the people who live here?" Mor said.

"They had to leave in a hurry. He was a policeman and was afraid he was going to be arrested. They fled to—I don't know where," Erik told Mor.

"Trust me, Margit, this is a safe house for now," Far said.

I ran from room to room ending in the bedroom where a huge bed stood all made up nice. I went back to the kitchen where Mor was washing down the counter with a wet rag.

"Look, here in the kitchen, there are dishes in the cupboards for you to use, Mama," Mor said, as she lit the pilot light on the water heater.

Zayde grabbed his suitcase and fumbled with the clasps to open it. Trying to help, Far jerked the suitcase from Zayde. Soon the two of them were in a tug a war over the luggage. The suitcase lid popped open and a load of pots and pans tumbled out, crashing to the floor.

"What the hell is this!?" Far asked. "Where are your clothes?" Far asked.

"*Rega, rega! Gey-kaken*, go away, Poul, and leave me alone!" Zayde yelled.

"Poul, they're kosher, they cannot cook or eat from any utensil that is not kosher," Mor said.

"This is too much, where are they going to get kosher food? They will have to eat what we get them."

"I can take care of that," Mor said.

"No, you can't. The Jews are no longer allowed to butcher animals and prepare meat according to Jewish law. The Germans have closed all their butcher shops. Erik and I will bring them their food. Don't worry, there will be no pork," Far sneered.

Mor bent down to help pick up the pots and pans. She slammed them down on the kitchen table to show Zayde she, too, was upset with Far for not understanding their Jewish ways.

We all went into the living room and sat in silence. Finally Far said, "As an extra precaution we must hang a tapestry near this window." He motioned to Erik, who opened a package wrapped in cloth and tied with twine. He held up a picture of the man with the halo over his head, like the one I'd seen in Hanne's Bible.

"Oh, my God," Mor cried and raised her hands to her face."

No, Poul, don't do this."

"Blasphemy!" shouted Zayde.

"Shut up, Margit. And make him understand. This will protect them if the Germans look in the window. They will think Danish Lutherans live here," Far said. "You must understand this—this is not a game! The German Gestapo is to be taken seriously. Your parents have to cooperate with this... their very lives depend upon it." He looked at Mor, his gray eyes were sharp. Tears flowed down Zayde's cheeks. "I'm an old man, what would the Germans want from me? How can I put another wife through another war? Poul, can't you understand, I'm tired of running."

"Old, young, it doesn't matter, just being a Jew is dangerous," Far told him.

"I guess, I guess, it is like me escaping from Russia many years ago and losing my first wife, killed by war. *Oy! Oy!* When will I be able to live in peace? Please take that picture out of here and leave us be," Zayde said, almost pleading with Far.

"Margit, tell your parents it stays! It must stay up!"

"God will forgive in these times, Papa," said Mor, trying to soothe him. "The Torah proclaims that in troubled times it is all right."

Zayde and Bubbe sat down and began to pray. They hugged each other as they did so.

Mor tried to comfort Zayde, but he waved her away.

"Let's get out of here, Poul. He will be thankful later," Erik said.

Far grabbed me and pulled me with him. We hurried down the stairs. Far's foot slipped and he fell and landed in a sitting position at the bottom of the stairs.

"Damn it to hell!" Far shouted. I landed on top of him. Getting right into my face, he said, "Johna, not a breath or a whisper to anyone about this house and who lives here, do you hear me!? No one is to know!"

Panicked with fear of Far's anger, I bit down on my tongue.

"*Ja,*" I said, feeling the pain in my tongue. "Another secret," I whispered, tears stinging my eyes.

"*Ja,*" said Far. Mor pulled me away from Far so he could

get up again. Then Erik picked me up and carried me down to the car.

"After I drop you off at home," he said to Far, "I'm going to pick up Alfred's girlfriend, Emma, and take her to the hospital to hide. She will hide as a Danish nurse. They will bleach her hair and give her a Danish name."

"Great, Erik. Thanks for taking care of it. We have to keep Alfred happy."

"Who is Alfred?" Mor asked.

"A friend that is helping us," Far answered. Mor stared at him, but he would not say anything more.

Back at home, Mor tucked me into the safety of my bed, and soon I went to sleep thinking of Bubbe and Zayde in their new home.

When morning came I heard hammering and jumped out of my bed and peeked around the corner of the door to see Far holding a hammer. He had taken off the hall doorframe and was stuffing papers and money in between the gaps of the wood. I watched him put the doorframe back into place and nail it down.

"Hi, Far," I said, moving past him on my way to the kitchen where Mor was fixing toast. I don't think Far knew that I had seen him hammering on the doorframe. I knew this was another secret I would have to keep, but I was tired of secrets and didn't want to ask.

"Mor, when can I go back to school?" I took the slice of toast from the stack and sat down at the kitchen table.

"I don't know, Little Skat."

"Would you buy me a red umbrella?"

"I'll talk to Far about it," Mor said, as Far came into the kitchen to pour himself a cup of coffee.

"What will you talk to me about, Margit?" Far sat down next to me.

"Johna wants her own red umbrella."

"An umbrella is an umbrella, red, blue, or black. Johna can use the one we already have."

"But it isn't red," I murmured.

"Red, why red?"

"Johna wants an umbrella like Hanne's, that's all," said Mor.

"Stupid! Why would she want to be a copycat? No! No, she can't have a red umbrella. That is final." He turned to talk to Mor. "Margit, I hid some money in case we would have to leave in a hurry, I'll tell you about it later." We were interrupted by the wail of air raid sirens.

"Why are there sirens in the middle of the day?" Mor asked Far as he looked out our living room window. Without waiting for an answer, she turned to me and said.

"Quick, Johna get dressed! Put on all those clothes," and pointed at the end of the bed. "It will be cold in the coal shelter. Hurry now!"

"Margit, I'm not going down to the cellar. I have to go meet Erik," Far said, and walked out the front door.

"Is Far not coming with us? I hope he won't get hurt from the boom, boom, boom of the bombs," I said. I thought of Zayde, and the cigar store man...and Hanne, and suddenly I was afraid. Everything was upside down. Nothing was the way it was before. I didn't know what to do, but had to stop it somehow. "I don't want to go to the dumb cellar," I cried out and ran away from Mor.

"Stop it, Johna. Why are you acting like this?" Mor screamed at me. She grabbed me, put me into my blue coat with the lumps of money in it, and led me downstairs to the coal cellar. Since it was morning, all my friends were at school and only adults were in the air raid shelter. I sat next to Mor and listened while she talked with Mr. Larsen.

"Margit, you must trust Poul," Mr. Larsen said. "He wants the best for your family and he will figure out what to do to keep you safe. People are angry over the news that Hitler wants to send all the Jews in Denmark to work camps. I have even heard talk of getting Danish Jews to safe ground."

"How do we know where is safe?" asked Mor.

"I am not real sure. The rumor is boats are gathering to sail all the Jews in Denmark across the sound to Sweden. We are hoping that they will welcome the Danish Jews." He looked down at me, and smiled. He reached into his pocket and pulled out a deck of cards. He held them out toward Mor. She nodded, and I watched them play cards while I ate cookies and colored in my coloring book. Finally, the all clear sounded in loud beeps to tell us it was now safe to go home.

Far was not there when we got back to the apartment. While Mor fixed lunch, I played with my paper dolls, pretending that they had to go to the air raid shelter. But their shelter was a beautiful room with bright pink silk curtains and white lace tablecloths on the long table that Far had built. Inside it was all the ice cream the dolls could eat and each one had a pretty red umbrella to keep it safe in case the roof fell in.

I was halfway through my liverwurst sandwich on pumpernickel bread when Far came in and sat across from me. He picked up a sandwich and ate a few bites, then washed it down with a bottle of beer.

"Far, can I pick up my sandwich with my hand and not use my fork and knife?"

"No, Johna!" he said.

Mor came into the kitchen. Far stood up to meet her. Then, taking her by the arm, he guided her into the bedroom and closed the door, leaving me alone at the table. I heard Far say something, and then she began to scream and sob. I opened the door to see what was the matter. Inside, Far had pulled a suitcase from under their bed and had laid it on the bedspread.

"Are we going on a trip?" I asked, and walked toward Mor.

Far turned in surprise at my question. "Get out, Johna," he said. Frightened, I backed away from Mor, but she grabbed me and put me on her lap. She kept crying and holding on to me. I was shaking. Far reached over and pulled me off Mor's lap and shoved me out the door. He slammed it behind me, but the latch didn't catch and it slowly opened again. I stood in front of the half-opened door to the bedroom, alone and confused, and wondered what I had done wrong to make Far so mad at me. Then I heard Far saying. "Margit, this is the only way. For your own safety, you need to hide out until I can make plans for all of us to get out of the country."

"Why can't I go live with my parents?" Mor asked.

Far saw me still in the doorway. He crossed over to me and shoved me out the door. "I said, get out!" he yelled, and again slammed the door behind me. I stood still by the bedroom door and listened to their yelling, tears filling my eyes, fear filling my stomach.

"I have made arrangements for you to hide out in Bispebjerg Hospital where many Jews using anonymous names are kept safe as Danish patients. I have also talked to Dr. Koester and we both feel it is best to perform an abortion.

"You can't make me kill this baby. I won't let you!"

"Margit, you've got to do this. There will be more babies later."

"Papa says that being pregnant again is God's goodness and mystery. Please don't make me do this, Poul!"

"Your papa thinks the messiah is coming, too. He's 82 years old and thinks he's a chosen man because he's a Jew. I have news for you both, his beliefs are just an old man's dreams."

"Yes," said Mor, raising her head in defiance, "they're his dreams, but his dreams are also for his grandchildren!"

"Well, he can keep his dreams to himself. Johna's a Christensen. A Dane, not a Jew! If we could keep this baby it would be a Dane, also.

Mor sobbed without control. "God is angry at my sin. I have shamed my parents. I lied to them about you being a Jew. We lied to your mother. She worked downstairs in the tavern and she left us alone in her apartment night after night, like I was one of her working girls. Now you want me to kill my baby. God will surely punish me this time. And what will happen to my Johna?"

"Killing a baby?" I whispered to myself. What could she be talking about?

"What about Johna," Far asked. "She has nothing to do with this!"

"If God punishes me, who will be her mother?"

"Margit, you're driving me nuts," said Far in exasperation. "It's true!"

"No! You're out of your mind. You need to get a hold of yourself."

"She will need a husband," Mor continued as if Far hadn't spoken. "How will she ever find a man who would want her? What kind of man would want a deformed wife?...damn you, Poul. It's a sin!"

"You are swearing now? Sin is only used to enslave and

deceive, and it robs those in this world by making promises that they hope will get them something in the next world. Your father can keep his beliefs to himself. Neither Johna nor I need the protection from a Hebrew God. It is for your health that you must get the baby out. We can't have a baby to worry about. It is too risky. What if you and Johna have to go into hiding and you are ready to give birth? Besides the hospital is a perfect cover from the damn Germans."

"Oy! Oy! Kill the baby. Noooooo!" I heard Mor yell and cry through the door.

"Margit, calm down. It's for the best."

"You're afraid that this baby may have a deformed hand like Johna. That's it. You don't want this baby."

"That's foolish talk. Your father blames her missing hand on me. I'm the scapegoat. How can he believe in a God who would punish a child? This is nonsense. Stop It! You're making me nuts. You're too emotional now." Far raised his voice, "Think straight! This is what's best for all of us."

"What will you do with Johna while I'm in the hospital?"

"She will stay with me and be safe. I'll see to that, don't worry. I will come to the hospital and we'll make plans to get us—and your parents—all out of Denmark."

My arms flailed up and down in front of my chest. The stork brings babies, I thought to myself. What does it mean to get rid of a baby if it has only one hand like me? Did they wish they had 'gotten rid' of me? Did it mean that the stork hadn't brought me? Was that why I only had one hand? Suddenly a fury came flooding through me.

"I hate you, Far!" I screamed as loud as I could, and stomped my feet. Far came to the door and looked at me, then he grabbed me. I struggled and kicked to get out of his strong hands. Just then a key clicked in the front door and Erik let himself in. Far let me go and I ran to Mor's arms.

"Let's go, Poul. Is Margit ready?" Erik asked, looking from Far to Mor and back to Far. Mor held me close and said through her tears, "I'm going to leave you with Far. I will be back soon, I promise." I clung to her with all my strength. It was more than I could bear.

When Erik pulled me away from Mor, I ran into the closet and opened my box of napkins. I removed the white dove napkin, held it in my teeth, and tore it into pieces. Erik, who had followed me into the closet, saw what I was doing and said, "Little Johna, don't worry, Mor will be fine. I wouldn't lie to you, would I?"

"I don't want her to go," I sobbed.

"I know, I know, but this is a necessary thing to keep you all safe. You want Mor to be safe, don't you?" He reached out and put his hand under my chin, turning it toward him. "Don't you?"

Slowly, I nodded my head.

"Good! Now, let's show your mor how brave you can be, OK?" He pulled me up and we went to wait by the door while Mor got her suitcase and coat. Then back we went down the stairs to the street and climbed into Erik's black car. Mor, holding her small suitcase on her lap, sat in the back with me, her hand clasping mine.

After a short drive into the country, Erik turned the car off onto a dirt road near a field where a white van with a Red Cross on the side sat. He pulled over and stopped. Far got out and took Mor's suitcase. Then he helped her out of the car. They walked slowly over to the ambulance, leaving me alone in the back seat of the car.

"Mor, don't go!" I yelled after her. Burning tears flooded my face and I trembled. I didn't even care if Far would be mad at me, I was crying for Mor. Erik climbed into the back seat, straightened the wrinkles in his suit, pulled out his hanky and polished the dust off his black shoes. Then he put his arm around me as we watched my parents walking toward the ambulance. Far opened the doors and a woman in a white uniform with a Red Cross on her white hat helped Mor into it. Mor turned and looked at me over her shoulder before she disappeared inside. I stood up to watch the van drive out of the field and onto the road. Sitting in the back of the car, I felt small and abandoned. I was so afraid I would never see Mor again.

"Johna," said Erik, touching my shoulder, "you must not tell anyone about Mor going to the hospital."

"Why?"

"It is all part of a game that we are playing. You can play a game, right?" Erik said, winking at me.

Just then, Far opened the car door and got into the passenger's seat. Erik left me alone in the back seat and got back behind the wheel.

"I don't like this game, Far," I complained.

"Mor will be coming home in a little while," Far said.

"In a little while? When is a little while?"

"Not too long," said Erik. "You play your part and be brave. If you wait and do just like Far tells you, we will win this game." I wondered if he was talking to me. I understood nothing.

Suddenly he swerved the car sharply onto a side street. I heard the tires squeal, and fell onto the floorboard as we slammed to a stopped. Far reached back and lifted me up to the front seat beside him. "You all right, Little Skat?" he asked, and hugged me close to him. Suddenly I didn't hate him anymore. I buried my face in his shoulder.

"I think a German truck followed us, Poul, but I think we lost them." Erik started the car again and we slowly moved in behind the ambulance and followed it the rest of the way to Bispebjerg Hospital. At the hospital I saw Mor climb out and get into a wicker wheelchair. She had her face buried in her white hanky as the nurse pushed her through the hospital doors.

"Mor! Mor!" I wailed as I saw my mother disappear.

"Johna, tell you what! Let's stop at Marie's Cookie and Ice Cream Stand and get you a big cone of French vanilla ice cream with strawberry jam on top," Erik said, smiling at me. "Mor is all right. She will be home soon, you'll see!"

"I do not feel like having an ice cream cone," I said with a whimper, but Erik didn't answer me. Instead he turned to Far.

"Poul, they are bringing Jews from all over and hiding them in the hospital. The whole staff is involved. Don't worry, this is the safest place for her. The code name for the hospital is 'the white brigade,'" Erik said.

"Ja, Ja, good," said Far.

That night I dreamt I was with Mor and Zayde, and we wrestled with lions. Then a nurse angel in a white uniform played a Jewish lullaby on Zayde's violin.

Chapter 11

Danish Resistance

I woke up early the next morning and looked over toward the big bed where Far lay alone, snoring softly. As I climbed into his bed, Far opened his eyes.

"You're awake," he said. "You can rest in my bed, while I fix us some bread and cheese for breakfast. Then I want you to dress quickly. We're going to Uncle Orla's pawnshop today." Uncle Orla was Far's older brother. He was taller than Far and had a trim brown mustache. He always wore nice gray suits. Sometimes Far visited Orla when Erik had something to pawn—or fence. The pawnshop he owned was the center for all kinds of extra-curricular business even before the Germans occupied Denmark. Afterwards, it was an easy transition to use those connections on behalf of the Danish resistance movement.

After breakfast, I opened the door of the bathroom where Far was taking a shower to ask him what clothes to put on. He turned off the shower and laid a towel on the wet floor, then stood on it in front of the mirror. Far smiled at me and said, "How is Far's pretty girl today?" He dipped his shaving brush into the shaving mug, making lather. I stood beside him as he looked into the mirror, watching the funny faces he made while shaving. He swirled his shaving brush in the mug and put some on my nose.

"Stop it, it tickles," I laughed.

When he finished shaving, he laid out the clothes for me to wear. Just then there was the sound of someone unlocking the front door, and Erik and my Uncle Arne entered. Uncle Arne was married to Far's sister, Ruth. He was tall and skinny. He owned a "Men's Corner," a casual clothing store on Amagerbrogade Street, and so always wore sporty clothes.

When Far was ready we all walked down the stairs and climbed into Erik's car. Erik gave me a bag of licorice. All his windows were rolled down, because the weather was warm so early in the morning. We passed bored German soldiers standing around smoking cigarettes and petting their guard dogs. Lots of people milled about the sidewalks, drawn out by the balmy weather.

Erik parked the car a block from the pawnshop on Langeline Street and rolled up the windows and locked the doors. He took my hand as I skipped along, trying to keep up with Far and Uncle Arne. We came to a halt as we waited for a German soldier pulling a large, two wheeled wooden cart to pass in front of us. Inside the cart were several people who looked like they were asleep. The soldier stared at me, making me uncomfortable.

"How did those people in the cart die, did you see the blood?" Far said.

"Hell, I have no idea what is going on or who they were," said Erik.

I looked up at Far in surprise, and turned back to where the soldier had been, but he had turned the corner by then and was out of sight.

"Far," I called out, "weren't those people sleeping?"

Far looked back over his shoulder at me. "*Ja*, Johna," he said, "they were sleeping all right."

At Uncle Orla's pawnshop, Far had his own key and unlocked the entrance. Inside were lots of knickknacks, old lamps, oriental rugs, fancy blue plates, and dolls on display, and all manner and kinds of things filled the many cupboards that stood around the walls. Uncle Orla was working at the counter near the back of the room. He looked up as we came in and waived at Far. As we walked over toward him, he pushed aside a green curtain that covered the entrance to another room. Inside were several men who stood beside a locked jewelry counter. Several others sat on an orange-flowered, three-pillow couch.

"Johna, come here to me," said one of them and I turned to see Thor Pehrrsen, Far's architect friend from Sweden. He sneezed, then said, "I have a present for you. I brought it from Sweden especially for you."

"What is it?"

"A Swedish doll—just for you. It has a full-flowered skirt like our girls wear at May Feast. I left it at the hotel, though, so I will get it to you later," Mr. Pehrrsen said. I tried not to show my disappointment at having to wait.

"Erik told me that Margit is in the hospital. How many Jews are hiding there?" Mr. Pehrrsen asked Far.

"I really don't know. No one must know too much. Margit and some other Jews are hiding in the lunatic ward. Some of them even look like lunatics," Far laughed.

I pulled at Far's trousers and he looked down at me. "Will the stork stop at the hospital and hide our baby?

"No, Johna, the stork is on strike!" Far said, and the others laughed.

"What's so funny, Far?"

"Johna, here...I have some chocolate milk for you," said Uncle Orla, and he hoisted me up on the glass counter.

"Chocolate, Orla? How did you find that?" Far asked.

"A friend got me some for my wife. She likes sweets," said Orla, setting out a glass. Then moved to the end of the counter where he had a small ice box, pulled out the jar of chocolate milk, and poured some for me.

"By the way, Poul, your mother tells me that you have some contacts among the Germans in her tavern. What is that about? You can't trust any of them, you know, Poul," said Uncle Arne.

"*Ja*, maybe," Far nodded. "I know that I must not trust anyone, but that doesn't mean we can't use them for our own purposes. Some Germans would like nothing better than to leave here and go home to their families, you know. "

Orla came back to where I was, lifted me down from the counter, and handed me my glass of chocolate milk. Just then, a small bell rang. Startled, I hid behind Uncle Arne, but then he walked back through the shop to answer the front door. I watched from behind the curtain and saw a man in black pants and turtleneck sweater in the doorway. He looked past Uncle Arne toward the men inside the back room.

"The man is here to pick up the ID cards and birth certificates," Uncle Arne shouted back to the others.

"Tell him to come back in an hour," Erik yelled back.

I walked over to the couch where the other men sat. They were gluing people's pictures on some papers. I was so interested, I didn't pay any attention to the glass of chocolate milk in my hand and it accidentally slipped out and spilled onto some of the photos.

"You stupid girl," a man standing by the couch yelled. I wanted to run away, but couldn't.

I just backed away from him, afraid of what he might do.

"Damn it, Poul! Kids have no place here," another man said, as he wiped the milk off the soiled papers. "Get Johna away from our work!"

Far came across the room and gave me a spanking on my behind. He took me by the arm and led me to the back of the shop and pushed me onto a big, gray, overstuffed chair that smelled old and dusty, then went back to where the men were gluing photographs. I looked around me. Across from me was a corner desk, behind which sat a bearded man counting money under the dull glow of a lamp. He looked over at me, but said nothing. Black curtains covered the windows here, just as they did at home. A fireplace stood at one end of the room. On its mantel sat a row of clocks ticking loudly. The smell of dust hung in the air, and the room was cluttered with boxes piled here and there and on top of one another.

"I want my Mor," I cried, and tears welled in my eyes.

"Just cuddle up in that chair and be quiet," the bearded man said. "Go to sleep."

I sat in that awful chair staring into space for what seemed a long while. Then all of a sudden, all the men from the other room crowded into the room with the bearded man and me. Erik and a couple of others moved to the windows and peeked carefully around the edges of the black curtains.

"Germans are all over the damn sidewalks," said Erik, watching from one corner. "They seem to be picking up Jews and making them go with them as if they were the dog catchers." He turned back toward the others who couldn't reach the window. "They're shoving them into the backs of trucks."

"Quick," said Far, "we need to get rid of the documents! Put the equipment into boxes and store them back there with the other boxes. If they come in here, first try to escape quietly out the back door, but if you can't, stand at the counter as if you are a customer," Far told the others.

Uncle Arne grabbed a newspaper off the floor. "Damn what are we going to do to hide this *Free Dane* paper?"

"Get rid of it. They'll know for sure it's the underground paper if they find it," Far said. He looked over at me, and then said, "Wait a minute! Give me that paper." He grabbed a pair of scissors off the desk where the bearded man sat and handed them to me. "Here, Johna," he said, "cut up this newspaper into tiny pieces. They'll not look at a child cutting up playthings."

"*Ja*, Far," I said, and began cutting the newspaper as he'd asked. Then I began ripping it up to make it go faster.

While everyone was running around hiding things, I called Far. "My hands are all dirty from the paper."

He picked up the shredded newspaper and stuffed it into a box on the floor and pointed to me. "Johna, you stay put in that chair, I'll be right back."

"It's clear now," said Erik, backing away from the window. "The Germans and their trucks drove off."

Far returned and washed my hands with a wet rag. He gave me more chocolate milk. It had a smell of whisky and made my insides all warm when I drank it. I soon fell asleep, remembering nothing else of our visit.

Chapter 12

Pigeon Resistance

By magic I awoke in my own bed to the alarm clock ringing and Far snoring loudly.

"Far, wake up!" I said, "The clock is ringing." I jumped out of my bed to see why he was still asleep.

Far woke, rolled over and moaned, "Oh, God damn it! I have an awful headache." Then he climbed out of his bed and staggered to the bathroom. I followed him. He had his head in the sink rubbing cold water on his face.

"Johna, you will come to work with me today, so go get dressed."

I quickly found a flowered yellow blouse and a purple skirt with a hole in it. I searched for matching socks but could only find two knee-highs, one light brown the other dark brown. After Far put on his white carpenter clothes, we went into the kitchen to eat some bread, butter, jam, and cut up cheese that we washed down with orange soda pop. Far looked at my clothes and laughed.

"Let's at least see what we can do with your hair," he said, and wet his comb to tackle my curls.

After that we hurried downstairs to Far's bike, as he kept saying he was late for work.

As we approached the Carlsberg Brewery where Far was working on a new warehouse they were building, I saw the huge stone elephants that stood guard on the sides of the entrance to the brewery. We went by them and through the brewery grounds until we stopped at the unfinished warehouse. Far parked his bike where others had left theirs and pulled me into the warehouse after him.

"Johna, I have to work now. You need to play by yourself for a while. Don't touch anything, and stay out of people's way," said Far, and headed off toward where several other men were starting to work.

I stood for a minute, looking around to see where I should

go, what I could do. After a while, I just wandered through the unfinished building looking for blocks of wood to build a bridge with. A boy a little older than I came over to play with me.

"I'll find a hammer and nails so your bridge will stay together," he said. He came back a moment later with a hammer and then we found some nails in the dirt. I watched him hitting the nails into the board.

"If you go get my father's hammer it will work better," I said. He just looked at me. Then he threw the hammer down. It hit my knee, hurting it. I began to cry and he ran off.

"Johna, why are you crying?" a voice asked. I looked up to see Steen Larsen, the pigeon man who worked with Far. I told him how the boy had hit my knee with the hammer.

"Let me see your knee," he said.

Just then Far came to find out what my crying was about. He bent down and took a look.

"It is not bleeding, just bruised," he said. "Little Skat, you're tough. No need to cry." He pulled me to my feet, saying, "Come, we're going home now."

All three of us left the building then. When we reached home Far stayed on his bike with one leg on the ground, holding the bike still while I climbed down.

"Johna, I want you to stay with Mr. Larsen until I get back. Mind him now."

"Come, little Johna," said Mr. Larsen, "I will put some medicine on your knee and we will go to the loft to feed the pigeons, how will that be?"

"*Ja*, Mr. Larsen," I said, feeling better at the thought of seeing the pigeons again.

With no wife to clean up, Mr. Larsen's apartment was a mess. He rummaged around and found some ointment to spread on the scratch on my knee. Then we climbed the curved back stairs to the loft, with me stopping to complain that my knee was hurting. But Mr. Larsen ignored my complaints and continued up to the loft. No one was washing clothes. I could hear pigeons cooing as we opened the washroom door. I limped onto the platform and watched the pigeons with their little red feet and their heads bobbing as they rushed to pick up the grain spread in their pen. A large gray pigeon fluttered outside the windowsill, trying to get in.

"Look, it's Edgar, I can't believe he's here, I thought I had lost him!" said Mr. Larsen, and he opened the window and grabbed the pigeon. He held the bird in the crook of his arm and removed a piece of oilskin paper from the leg bracelet. He stuffed the note into his pocket and turned to me.

"How would you like to send a note to your mother at the hospital?" he asked. In answer, I jumped up and down and pulled on his arm. "Calm down," he laughed. "What do you want to say to your mother?"

"Tell Mor to come home."

"*Ja, ja*, I will do that for you." He grabbed a big white and black pigeon that was resting on the roost. He pursed his lips, wetting the stubby pencil on his tongue and wrote the note. Then he rolled the note and put it in the small tube that was attached to the pigeon's leg. "Shoo, shoo, little bird," he said, and opened his hands to let it fly away into the clear blue sky.

"This bird will go to the tower next to the hospital and a nice nurse will give the note to your mother."

"Good bird. Will you take me to go see Mor, Mr. Larsen?"

"We will ask Far when he gets back," he said.

Just then I heard something and turned to see Far reaching the top rung of the ladder to the loft.

"Far! I wrote a note to Mor and the pigeon will give it to her," I said, jumping up and down pulling on his arm.

"God damn it, Steen! You idiot, have you lost all your marbles? She is just a kid who has enough secrets to keep."

"Ha! She already knew. Stop being such a horse's ass and don't talk to me like that. It is stupid to argue over it now." Mr. Larsen said, turning away.

"You are a damn fool, Steen—you blunder like a nincompoop and make yourself a danger to the Danish resistance."

"Shut the hell up, Poul!" said Mr. Larsen, his face red with anger. "Let's just get on with our work." He pulled out a large soiled handkerchief and wiped tobacco spit from his mouth.

Their angry words troubled me. I didn't know why they

were yelling at each other, and I couldn't understand why Far was mad at me for writing a note to Mor.

Far opened a small package he was holding. Soon the two of them were busy writing notes and stuffing them in the birds' tubes. I helped take the birds out one at the time. Then they let the pigeons loose, sending them out of the hatch window and into the clouds. Below us we heard someone in the washing room.

"Let's go home now, Johna. We are done here," said Far.

At our apartment Mr. Larsen and Far shared a beer and listened to the radio news. I went into the bedroom and checked my windowsill to see if the sugar cube was still there and wondered when the stork would bring our baby.

Chapter 13

Swastika Allies

The next morning I was playing in the living room when Far came out of the bedroom all dressed up in his suit and blue tie.

"Come on, Johna, let's get you dressed. We're going to Farmor's café for lunch." He took special care in my clothes this time, and laid out my yellow blouse, brown halter with pleated skirt, white lace ankle socks, and my black patent leather shoes. He even tied a yellow bow in my hair.

"Where's our camera?" Far asked.

"I can find it for you," I said. I liked showing him things that I knew he didn't know. In a moment I had found it and given it to him. Then we were ready to go. It felt good to be going out with Far, as if we were going to a party. For a little while it made me forget that Mor had gone, and all the other strange and disturbing things that had happened over the last few weeks.

When Far and I arrived at the train station, we found it was closed. German Gestapo soldiers with dogs stood guard at the train gate.

"Damn it to hell!" Far said, looking at them through narrowed eyes.

The soldiers were laughing at the way passersby shied away each time their guard dogs barked and growled at them, lunging and straining on their leashes. Far didn't even stop, but instead headed across the street toward the trolley. After we got on, I kept my head down and looked at my feet, as Mor had told me to do.

As we neared our stop, Far stood up and held my hand, getting ready to get off. Then the brakes squealed and the trolley came to a sudden stop, throwing us forward. At the same time, the doors opened and Far fell into a soldier standing by the door. The soldier shoved Far so hard that he fell out onto the sidewalk, letting go of my hand and landing on his butt. I jumped down off the trolley after him, being careful not to touch the German soldier. I stared at Far lying on the ground.

"I must have slipped," Far mumbled.

I didn't understand this. Why didn't he hit the soldier or even yell at him, I wondered.

The rest of the passengers were quiet and no one moved to help Far. The trolley driver closed the doors and it rumbled on down the street. It was then I looked around and saw that we had gone in a different direction than toward Farmor's.

"Why are we going this way, Far? Farmor's is the other way," I said. Far picked himself up off the street, dusting his pant legs with his hand.

"I just want to look at last night's bombings and go down to the boat pier so we can take some pictures."

We walked toward the black smoke I could see rising in the distance. Soon we came to the railroad yard, where smoldering, overturned boxcars and engines were scattered on top of twisted tracks and broken railroad ties. Fire still licked at the sky, and thick smoke drifted over the warehouses and other buildings, filling the air with a bad smell.

"Johna, don't move and I will take a photo of you." Far motioned me to stand in front of the wrecks and the smoke. "That's it," he said. His camera clicked. Three blocks farther we came to a large building where we could see flames burning inside. Shattered glass covered the road and the smell of burning wood drifted around us. Far stopped and took another picture of me. In this fashion, we continued towards the pier where the smell of oil and smoke hung in the air.

Out in the harbor I could see ships with water over their decks, and smaller boats floating upside down. Here, too, heavy smoke curled skyward. From time to time, flashes of orange flame burst from the boats.

"Johna," said Far, putting his hand on my shoulder, "when you go to the coal cellar to be safe, this is what is happening. These ships weren't so safe." He pointed toward the broken ship.

"That's the *Wartheland*, a German ship the Danes sank," he said.

"Why do you sink a ship?" I asked.

Far didn't answer. Instead he walked over to a man seated on the pier repairing a fishing net.

"What is happening over there?" Far asked him, and nodded toward a large vessel where German soldiers hurried between the ship and the pier. The fisherman continued weaving a bobbin in and out of his net, answering without looking up.

"Jews are in the hold of that ship," he said. "The Germans are arresting Jewish Communists, that's what they call them, anyway, and shipping them off to work camps."

Seeing the soldiers guarding the docks, made me tense and I began to chew on my fingernails. Far pulled his watch out of his pocket and took a look at it. After he put it back, he lifted me up on his shoulders and we walked toward a park just down the street from the harbor.

"When are we going to Farmor's?" I asked.

"Pretty soon, Johna. But before we go to Farmor's, you can feed the ducks and swans in Søndre Park." Far stopped at a vending stand at the entrance of the park and bought bread for me to feed the ducks.

Far sat down on a bench facing away from the water, and I ran to the lake where the ducks huddled on the shore. I looked back to make sure Far was still at the bench and saw two bikes stop in front of Far's bench. On one was Alfred, Far's German officer friend from Farmor's, and on the other was a lady who had a swastika pinned to her blouse.

I left the ducks at the lake and came up and hid behind Far.

"Alfred, you're on time," said Far, putting his watch back into his pocket.

"This must be Johna," said the woman. "She's so cute."

Far turned over his shoulder to see where I stood and motioned me forward.

"Johna, this is Myra," he said, pointing to the lady. She offered me her hand, but I backed away and just curtsied. Myra was very skinny and had short, red, wavy hair and smelled of perfume. She folded her arm inside my father's bent elbow and smiled up at him. They seemed to like each other.

"I am glad to see you again, Myra," said Far, putting his arm around her waist and hugging her. He let his hand slip to her butt. "I've missed you. I don't go to the German Nazi Party anymore."

"I have been gone anyway. In only just returned from

Germany, Poul, and heard the news about deporting Jews," said Myra.

"That's not good news for my family," said Far.

Alfred interrupted the conversation. "I asked you to meet me here, Poul, for a reason. You have to come up with some money, *ja*? Our contacts want to get paid for risking their necks to help Jews."

"Are you asking for a bribe, Alfred?"

"That's how it is," said Alfred. "Listen, I have to go now. We can't be caught talking for too long. See you at the tavern, Poul...just get the money," he said, as he got back on his bicycle.

Far bent down and kissed Myra on the lips. Myra took out a lace hankie and wiped her lipstick off his mouth. The hankie had blue thread on the borders and a swastika in the corner, just like the hankie that Far had used to wipe the ice cream from my face on that night in my bed.

Alfred and Myra rode on down the path and out of the park.

"Why did you kiss her, Far?"

"Just never mind, Johna. We are now on our way to eat a good meal at Farmor's." I didn't understand this kissing business, but I knew I wouldn't get anything more out of Far and to push it would only anger him.

As we walked nearer to Farmor's, I could see the neon light that read "Absolan Café." Two old men in baggy pants and grubby clothes leaned against the building. They both held wine bottles close to their chest. Ladies in short, tight, halter dresses leaned from the windows of the second floor and waved to us. Instead of going in the front, however, we turned down the back alley to the kitchen door.

Inside the kitchen, Farmor stood with her back to us, stirring a steaming pot on the stove and frying pork chops. I saw one of the raw pork chops fall from her hand and drop to the floor. She picked it up and rinsed it off under the waterspout and then threw it back into the frying pan. I came up behind her and hid at her back. She swung her hand behind her and grabbed me, making me giggle.

Farmor always smelled like brandy and the cigars she smoked. Sometimes, when she got too close, the hot ashes of her cigar would drop on me, burning my arm or making holes in my clothes.

"You hungry, Johna?" she asked. "How about a plate of *frikadeller* meat balls?"

Before I could even answer, she lifted me onto a tall stool at the kitchen counter. People bustled all about the kitchen, preparing food. Too many things were going on for Farmor to pay much attention to me.

"Son, why are you not at work?" Farmor asked Far.

"I've taken a vacation, Mother," said Far.

"How can you afford to do that?"

"I make enough, and don't worry, I haven't forgotten that I owe you money. I just need a little time to pay you back...but right now I need some more cash to help Margit."

"*Ja, Ja*, right," said Farmor as she flipped the pork chops and stirred the soup again.

"...And how is Margit?"

"She's still in the hospital."

"Is she all right?" she asked, looking over her shoulder at Far.

"*Ja, Ja*, she's fine," said Far.

"And the baby?" asked Farmor.

"Margit lost it."

"Mor lost it?" I popped in on their conversation. "How can Mor lose a baby? The stork will find it, won't it? Far?" Far looked at me and scowled, as Farmor leaned over and gave me a kiss.

"She'll be in the hospital for a few days, but you are not to visit her, Mother—not that you would have time for that," Far said. "Having a baby right now is dangerous for her."

"This is about the Jews, isn't it? Can Margit's father help with money?"

"No, Mother."

"Jews always say they have no money and always find some when they need it," Farmor said.

"Let's go have a beer, Mother," said Far, moving toward the bar and motioning to Farmor to follow him.

"We'll have a beer in a minute, young man," Farmor hissed. If you hadn't married a Jew, you would not have the problems you are having now."

"That's not your concern," said Far, his voice growing sharp. "I'm having to come up with some cash right now, or there will be troubles for me."

"I'll get you some more money, but my concern is for Johna. She's my first-born granddaughter, regardless of the rest of her family. Why don't you leave her here to live with me? My maid Marie can watch her when I can't."

"Mother, I'm not leaving her here."

"Poul, your friends in the resistance and the Germans that are helping you are too dangerous for Johna," said Farmor.

"My friends! Look at you! Look at this place—it's packed with Germans! Without them you wouldn't make a dime. You'd be shut down," said Far, waving his arm in a circle.

"Shut up, Poul. I'm your mother, and I won't have you talk to me like that! If it weren't for my German customers, I wouldn't have the money I have to loan to you. Remember when you believed in Hitler? It wasn't that long ago. The Germans have been good for my business. A smart Dane knows how to butter her own bread," said Farmor, and shook her tongs at him.

"I'm disappointed with the iron hand that the Nazis have begun to rule with. The German occupation has changed since they first came three years ago. I am not a puppet on a string, and the Jews have done nothing to deserve being treated like this."

"Well, it's sad that you have married a Jew. Such helpless, exposed people, even if they are Danes," said Farmor.

"Johna's best part comes from our family, Mother. She has spunk. She's more like me than her mother," said Far.

"And you are more like your father than me, floundering around like a drunken alley cat, always chasing women when you have a wife."

"What do you mean?"

"Have you forgotten your Nazi girlfriend, Myra? Who in the hell do you think you are?"

"Myra is not a true Nazi."

"Looks like a duck, walks like a duck," said Farmor.

"I need a woman who doesn't run off at the drop of a hat to a Synagogue to be with her parents," said Far.

"And Margit needs a husband who doesn't run off with

another woman," Farmor shot right back.

"What she doesn't know won't hurt her. I only married her so she wouldn't have to raise Johna with her deformed arm all alone," said Far. As he said this, I dropped my left arm down under the table, but as I did so, I hit the edge of my plate, tipping it. Meatballs and gravy spilled across the table and onto Farmor's shoes.

"Damn it, Johna!" Far yelled and he raised his hand at me.

"Don't you touch her! It's not her fault you don't know how to control yourself. Take her into the tavern. Order some more food and cool off!" Farmor yelled at him, and her long, skinny cigar fell from her mouth onto the counter.

"*Ja, Ja!*" Far said, and raised his hands at Farmor and shrugged his shoulders.

The tavern was crowded, but Far seemed to know everyone. Many German soldiers waved at him.

"*Skål,*" they all yelled at Far, holding their drinks in the air. We sat down at a crowded table. One of the waitresses immediately brought over a pitcher of beer for Far and his friends, and a glass of milk for me. The room smelled of tobacco smoke and good food. Alfred and Myra were already there and pulled up some chairs to join us. We sat for a while and listened to the piano man playing and singing funny songs for the crowd. Then Far pulled me up from my chair.

"Johna, get up on the table here and sing the song I taught you," he said. I jumped up on the table and Far motioned to the piano player to start playing.

"I'm a pretty girl," I sang, "and I can dance and do tricks for you and spend the money you could have saved for beer." As I sang, some of the soldiers tossed coins on the table at my feet. They all clapped and laughed.

"She is a little Shirley Temple," Farmor said, coming up just as Far was collecting the coins.

After my song, Far sat me down again, but I didn't want to be there with Alfred and Myra anymore, so I slipped under the table and went over to the cloakroom where Marie, Farmor's maid, was hanging up the customer's coats. She smiled at me as I moved in and out between the coats, checking the pockets for candy. Then my yellow bow caught on a button on a German Uniform. I was struggling to free my hair, when I felt a strong hand grab my arm.

"You little thief! Looking for money, eh?" said a large German soldier. Before I could even answer, he hit me across my face. My glasses went flying off my nose. It was mean Carl, Alfred's friend, the one I had seen upstairs the last time we had been at Farmor's.

"FAR! FAR! FAARRR!!!!" I screamed. Far ran from the table and jumped over the cloak room counter. In one movement, he drove his fist into Carl, sending him to the floor.

"*Sie Sheisskopf!*" (You Shithead) Carl yelled from the floor.

"Don't you ever hit her again, or you will not see daylight!" Far shouted at him.

"Stop! Both of you!" Alfred came around the counter. "It was just a mistake, Poul! Right Carl?"

"*Ja, Ja*, I thought she was stealing," said Carl, as he picked himself up and brushed off his uniform.

The crowd gathered around them and laughed, but Alfred waved them away. Far and Carl exchanged threatening glances, but under Alfred's look, Carl went back to his table.

When Carl was gone, I ran to Marie. "Far, I want to stay here with Marie," I said. I loved Marie, and thought she was beautiful. She always wore a short black dress with a frilly apron with pockets, where she kept her tips. She took good care of me whenever I was at Farmor's.

"That will be all right, Little Skat," said Far. He picked up my unbroken glasses from the floor and placed them back on my face. "You stay here with Marie."

I watched Marie pick up the fallen coats. A gun lay next to the wall. I grabbed it, slipped it under my skirt, and ran to the kitchen, where I ran right smack into Farmor's rear end.

"Look," I said, pointing it at her, "I found a gun!"

"Don't point that at me, Johna! Where did you get that?" Farmor snatched the gun from my hand and looked at Far, who had just followed me into the kitchen.

"Why does Johna have a gun?"

"You don't want to know, Mother! And be quiet! Do you

want everyone to hear?" Far said. "I think it belongs to Carl. It fell out of his holster. He's too drunk to notice, but I must get this back to him. We don't want any more trouble."

Far took my hand and we walked slowly back to the cloak-room, where he handed Marie the gun and whispered a few words to her. Then Far brought a beer and a whisky over to Carl. I held on tightly to Far's arm, not wanting to go near Carl again. To my surprise, Carl smiled at me and gave me money. I was too scared to refuse, so I took it from him. Marie came over to Carl and whispered something to him. Carl giggled and reached for his gun holster and froze, finding it empty. Before he could say anything, Marie laughed and handed him the revolver.

We returned to our table and ate some open-faced sand-wiches and pea soup. When we had finished, Far and Myra got up. Far motioned to me and the three of us left Farmor's together. We walked down the street a little way, then Far took us into a hotel, where he rented a room. Once in the room, Far gave me a drink of whisky in a soda and put me to bed on the couch. Before I went to sleep, I heard Myra and Far whispering and laughing in bed. Right then, more than anything, I wanted Mor.

Chapter 14

Hiding Places

The next morning Erik came to the hotel door. He'd come to tell us things had changed again on the streets of Copenhagen. The Germans had intensified their ambitions for the Danish Jews. This had not gone as well as planned, for the Danish people had followed the counsel of their king. Erik was very excited and talking fast.

"Poul, the German's have been stopping everyone on the street that they think might be Jews. They make them sit on a fire hydrant that hurts their butts until they confess they are Jews. Then they give them a Star of David patch and order them to sew it onto their clothes, so that they are identified at all times.

"But you know what King Christian did? He declared that all Jews are Danes, so all Danes should wear the Jewish patch. So many have done so that the Gestapo police knew they were beaten and they stopped passing out the patches." Erik shook his head and laughed. "The Germans are really pissed," he finished.

"*Ja*, that is good news," said Far. "I can see why they would be pissed."

"That's not all, though," Erik continued. "They arrested the Danish police and took them away to who knows where."

"I wonder if they arrested Neils Strum...you know, my neighbor downstairs. He's a Danish police officer. This is not good."

While Far and Erik talked about what the Germans were doing, Myra lit a cigarette and came over to me. She had gathered up her things and was preparing to leave. She tried to give me a hug good-bye, but I turned away from her. Far saw me do this and interrupted his conversation with Erik.

"Johna, what's the matter with you?" he said. "Give Myra a hug."

"Oh, Poul, she is just shy," said Myra, much to my relief. Without saying anything more to me, she put on her coat. Far hugged her and gave her a quick kiss. Then Myra turned and walked toward the door, waving once as she left.

After Myra left, Erik drove Far and me home. As the three of us climbed the stairs to our apartment, Mrs. Johnsen, Mor's Jewish friend from upstairs, met us on the stairs. She was also agitated, but not in the excited way Erik had been. Mrs. Johnsen was frightened.

"Poul! There you are!" she said, reaching toward him. "The Germans have been here, knocking on all doors to see if we we're hiding Jews. Somehow they passed up my door. I'm so afraid—my aunt and uncle are hiding in my clothes cabinet. What if the Germans come back and find them?" she asked, clutching Far's arm.

"Just stay calm," said Far, and put a hand on her shoulder. "I will come up to see you later, all right?"

"Ja, Ja," she said, nodding her head and looking back up the stairs toward her apartment.

"Oh, and could you watch Johna tomorrow?" Far asked.

"Ja, sure, that's fine," said Mrs. Johnsen.

Inside our apartment, Erik and Far whispered with one another. Then Far pushed me towards the kitchen. "Go get us a beer, Johna."

When I came back, Erik took the beer, then waving his bottle at us, he headed toward the door. "Have fun with Far," he said to me as went out the door.

Far turned to me. "Johna," he said, "let's play a game of you hiding and I will find you."

"Are you going to play a game with me?" I asked, not believing my ears.

"Yes, you'll hide in the cedar chest."

"That's not hiding," I said, "because you'll know where I am."

"We are going to pretend someone else is looking for you."

"Who would I hide from?" I asked, mystified by this game.

"From whoever comes and knocks on our door. You just crawl inside this chest and be quiet and very still, understand?" said Far, opening the lid to the big cedar chest with the carvings on the side.

"Are the Germans looking for me, Far?" I asked, thinking of what Mrs. Johnsen had said on the stairs about the Germans looking for Jews, and sometimes I was a Jew.

"Neighbors, Germans...we are hiding from everyone," said Far. "I want you to climb into the chest and close the lid and stay there until I come and get you out."

"But why I should hide?" I asked, starting to be afraid, like Mrs. Johnsen.

"Don't worry, Little Skat," said Far, squeezing my shoulder, "this just a game. I will always be there to get you out."

"But Far, only Jews hide. You told me that I am not a Jew anymore. I don't like this game."

"Stop it, Johna. Just do it for Far, and I will give you a sip of beer when I come to get you out after the game is over."

"*Ja*, Far," I said, afraid to push Far's temper.

Far went to the door and knocked. The lid of the chest was heavy, but I managed to open it enough to squeeze my body into the chest. The lid closed behind me with a bang. Then I waited. It was very dark and creepy inside the chest, and hard to breathe. I wanted to get out, and worried that I could not lift the heavy lid by myself. Soon, however, Far came and opened the lid.

As he helped me out I clung to him, happy to see him.

"I was afraid, Far. It was so dark and I couldn't breathe!"

"I told you I will always come and get you. Be a brave girl now," said Far, and hugged me to him. He crossed to the table and picked up his beer, handing it to me for a sip.

"You were a good girl, Johna. You did that perfectly. Now we will try it again, and this time put the sheets on top of you so no one can see you if they open the lid, then lie very still. If the lid opens, do not move unless I talk to you, understand? Don't move unless you hear me speak to you."

"*Ja*, Far, I understand," I said, though I didn't understand at all. I just knew to do what he told me to.

"Now this time, when there's a knock, tiptoe to the chest and get in—be quiet as a mouse. Shh," said Far, putting his finger to his lips.

"Shh," I whispered back.

Far sat in his chair by the radio and I went to sit on the small stool next to him and waited to play the game. Soon Far knocked on the table by his chair, and I tiptoed to the chest. I had trouble lifting the lid again, but Far helped me and I climbed inside. I rustled around for the sheets to cover me. I pulled them up over me as Far had said, and made a nest for my face so I could breathe better. Even so, it was so warm and stuffy. I soon started to squirm.

What was taking so long, I wondered. Where was Far? My legs were hurting and I want to get out. Finally I heard the lid open, but remembering what Far had said about not moving until he said so, I held my breath and didn't move.

"Little Skat, it's me" he said. He reached in and touched me under the sheets. I wiggled free from the sheets as fast as I could, desperate to get out at last. Far picked me up and lifted me out of the chest. It hurt to unbend my legs, and I had been in the darkness so long that the light of the room hurt my eyes. Far closed the lid and we sat down on top of the chest and together sipped his beer.

"Can I hide under the bed instead?"

"No, Johna," Far laughed, " You cannot hide under the bed."

In the quiet of the room, the hall clock pendulum clicked back and forth. It was so peaceful I laid my head on Far's lap, but it wasn't long before I thought of Mor in the hospital.

"Far, did the Germans take the stork and our baby away?"

"Damn it, Johna, the stork isn't coming here. There's no baby, so forget the baby."

"The stork won't come here?"

"No."

"Then will the stork come to the hospital where Mor is? Can I put the sugar cube there?"

"No!"

I got so mad at that, that I went into the bedroom, climbed up on my bed by the window, took the sugar cube from off the window sill and ate it.

Just then there was a knock at the door. I ran back to Far, not knowing for sure what I should do.

"Hide in the chest, quick now!" Far whispered as he came out of the kitchen. Frightened, I had trouble opening the lid again, but Far helped me into the chest. I got tangled up in the sheets and tablecloths. Finally, I found I was more comfortable by turning on my side. I lay still inside, listening. Someone in heavy boots had come in and I could hear them shuffling around the room, accompanied by muffled voices. The footsteps moved closer. I froze. I have to be brave, I thought. I squeezed my eyes shut and wished with all my heart the whoever was there would not look in the cedar chest.

The footsteps came toward me, then stopped. I held my breath until it hurt. Then they moved away again. More than anything I wanted Mor. I felt like I was going to cry, but Far had said I must be quiet. And so I waited inside the chest, holding back my tears, for what seemed like forever.

Then, suddenly, the lid opened. As light filled the opening, I saw Far's face above me through a peak hole in the tablecloth that lay over me. He reached down and lifted me out. I held onto him so tight. I looked all around the living room then, but Far was alone, except for me. He wiped the sweat from my face with a white linen napkin.

It was then I noticed the room smelled of cologne, like the kind Alfred used.

"You are a good, girl," said Far, and wiped his own eyes with the napkin. He leaned over and kissed me, then handed me his beer. I took three sips of beer instead of one.

"Far, I don't know how to be brave," I said, starting to tell him how hard it had been in the chest, but just then I saw my dollhouse was gone. "Who was here? Where is my doll house?" I blurted out.

"Just someone who wanted to help us play the game of hide and seek and to buy your dollhouse," Far said.

"My doll house is gone!" I looked on the floor where one of my very small dolls lay on the floor. "What did you do with it?"

"I will build you another," Far said.

"I don't want another one!" I said, all my fear turning into anger. "When is Mor coming home? I want Mor back!" I shouted. Mor wouldn't have given my dollhouse away.

"Shh, Johna. We'll go and see her soon, I promise. I have a Danish ID card for you to show to any grown-up or a German soldier who wants to see it. I will carry it for you. See it has your picture on it. If they ask you if you are a little Jewish girl, you say 'no.'"

I looked at the picture on the card and learned that lying about being a Jew was part of the hide-and-seek game.

The rest of the evening Far taught me how to play poker. He won most of the time and took away the pennies that he had given me to play the game. This was too much for me and when I got into a snit about it, he sent me to bed.

"May I sleep with the light on tonight?"

Far smiled at me. "Just tonight, Johna."

The next morning Far was searching through all the cupboards, looking for something to make for our breakfast. All he found was some old bread, which we ate with butter, and we drank the last of the milk.

"Today you're staying most of the day with Mrs. Johnsen, "Far said.

"I want to go with you!"

"No, Johna, you can't go with me. But here's what I want you to do...I want you to hide in Mrs. Johnsen's secret closet whenever someone knocks on her door. It's just like the trunk game we played yesterday. Her Jewish aunt and uncle will be in the closet with you, so you won't be alone. But remember, if someone knocks on Mrs. Johnsen's door, you do as you are told."

After breakfast, Far took me upstairs to Mrs. Johnsen. They exchanged a few words and then he left. I watched him walk out the door and felt so alone.

"Johna, your father says you are good at keeping secrets," Mrs. Johnsen said.

"Ja, I know a lot of secrets."

"Secrets are much a part of our lives now, aren't they, little Johna?"

I wasn't sure what she meant by that, but I followed her into her bedroom to a large cabinet with two mirrored doors. She opened one door and pushed aside her clothes. Mrs. Johnsen knocked three times on the back panel in the closet. The panel opened slowly, and then two people crawled out from the closet. I could smell their sweat. They blinked at the bright lights, and tried to straighten their stiff legs to stand up.

"Close your mouth, little girl," the man said to me. I moved closer to Mrs. Johnsen. The man looked like Zayde with

122

his long beard and yarmulke, but he wasn't at all like him. He wore wrinkled black trousers, a tattered gray sweater with missing buttons. He had no shoes on his white feet. The woman looked sleepy and her hair was black and matted. She was also shoeless, though she had on thick brown stockings. A gray and black shawl hung over her shoulders.

"I can't believe that this mere child knows of this closet," the lady said to Mrs. Johnsen.

"How could you expose us to her? How could you do such a thing?!" she said, anger filling her words.

The man pointed his finger at me, then brought his stiff-bearded face to mine. I could smell his bad breath.

"You better not tell anyone about us here or the bad police will come and punish you," he said, shaking his finger in my face.

"There is no need to frighten the child," said Mrs. Johnsen. "She knows how to keep secrets. Don't you, Johna?"

"*Ja*, Mrs. Johnsen," I replied, trying to keep from shaking.

"This is Johna," she said to the two. "Her grandfather is Yechiel Pressmann, the tailor."

"Yes, he has sewn some things for me," the man answered.

"Let's go to my kitchen and find something to eat and drink," Mrs. Johnsen said. They left me alone by the closet. I crawled into the open hole in the closet. I picked up a flashlight that lay beside the hole and turned it on to see where they had come from. Inside the hole was a mattress, blankets, pillows, as well as bottles of water, books, boxes of crackers, and a smelly piss pot.

"Johna! Come here!" Mrs. Johnsen called from the kitchen. I crawled back out from the closet and went to the kitchen. Mrs. Johnsen was dishing out potato soup for all of us. She gave us each a dark piece of bread with nothing on it.

"I don't like this soup or bread," I said. "Can I have something else?"

"No, you eat what I serve you," said Mrs. Johnsen, as she sipped at her cup of tea.

I made a face, but nibbled at the bread. "Can Mor come and hide in the closet?"

"There wouldn't be room, but don't worry, we'll have a space for you to hide."

"But I'm not a Jew anymore, and I don't have to hide," I said, not telling about how Far had wanted me to hide in the chest.

"Now she is ashamed of being a Jew. Oy, Oy, what is this world telling this poor child of God," the man said. "She's all mixed up about being a Jew."

"Don't worry," said Mrs. Johnsen, "her father is just making sure she is silent."

"We will have to do a lot of praying to make sure of that," the bearded man said, and shook his finger at me again.

After we all finished eating our soup, the man and woman returned to the closet. I stayed in the apartment with Mrs. Johnsen.

"I will read you a story from Hans Christian Anderson," she said, and motioned for me to sit down on the sofa. She began to read to me, but after she finished I couldn't even remember any of her words from the storybook. They all just fell around me without making any sense. She got up to go into the bathroom. I followed her and watched her wash her bra in the sink.

For some reason, I started to just talk, saying whatever words came into my head. "My friend Hanne and I sometimes pretend that she is a Jew," I said. "We put a handkerchief on our heads and rock back and forth and make up silly prayers. I am also getting a red umbrella someday."

She told me to stop the chatter. She finished up in the bathroom and then went back to the living room. I followed her back into the dimly lit room. Bored, I lay down on the floor and soon fell asleep.

In the early evening, the air raid siren wailed.

"Johna, get up and get into the closet," said Mrs. Johnsen.

"No, I don't want to go in there. It stinks and I don't like the people in that closet," I said, and ran to the opposite corner of the room from her.

"Wait till your father hears how badly you are behaving," Mrs. Johnsen said. But I didn't care and wouldn't go. Finally she gave up trying to get me to.

"Hurry to the shelter," the air raid warden yelled from the hallway, banging on the door with a stick. Mrs. Johnsen and I rushed down to the coal cellar. We sat down at the first space we came to at the long table and when I looked up, Hanne and her mother were sitting across from us. Hanne saw me and waved to me as if she weren't mad at me anymore. I smiled and returned her wave, but seeing Hanne again only made me sadder that we didn't play together anymore. People had brought food into the shelter and a pile of sandwiches and some fruit sat on the table in front of me. I was hungry, so I grabbed an egg sandwich and a red apple. Hanne and I both reached for the food at the same time and this made us laugh. It was just like we were friends again.

"Where is Johna's mother?" Hanne's mother asked Mrs. Johnsen.

"Margit is on a short holiday and Poul is working and asked me to look after Johna," Mrs. Johnsen said.

"Strange time for Margit to go on a holiday trip without Poul or Johna. But I guess that is none of my business," Hanne's mother replied. Mrs. Johnsen ignored her comment.

It was two days before Far came back for me. When he did, his face was covered with bruises and scratches.

Mrs. Johnsen gasped when she saw him. "Poul, what happened? Are you all right?"

"Ja, Ja, I couldn't get back sooner. Some fool exploded a phosphorous bomb behind a nightclub bandstand. I threw a pitcher of beer on the fire and it burned even worse. It was a complete mess, bottles breaking everywhere, people screaming. A lot of folks got hurt, even a few Germans. The Gestapo arrested Erik and me. We spent the night being interrogated at the Dagmar prison. Late this afternoon, Alfred, a friend of mine got us released.

"My goodness, how awful," Mrs. Johnsen said. Then before Far said anything more, she blurted out, "I can't watch Johna anymore, don't ask me."

"All right, Mrs. Johnsen. Good-bye," Far said, and took my hand. We left Mrs. Johnsen without a backward glance or even a thank you.

Chapter 15

Shots in the Park

With Far home I felt much better. He slept most of the day that first day, but awoke now and then to make us something to eat and to put medicine on his wounds. I wandered around the house, playing with my paper dolls and at my imaginary game with the carvings on the cedar chest. Peeking out from behind the black-colored drapes, I wished I could go outside and didn't have to hide. I thought about how nice it would be if Hanne were here to play with me.

It was getting dark outside when Far got up. He turned the light switch on and dressed in a black sweater and trousers.

"Johna, here, put on your dark ski pants and your coat. Hurry now," Far said.

"But it's not cold or snowing!" I said, surprised by what he wanted.

"Just do what I say, damn it." Far's tone warned me to shut up.

When I was dressed, Far led me out to the street where Erik waited in his car, his motor running. His windshield wipers clicked back and forth in the rain. No sooner had we climbed in, than Erik stepped on the gas pedal. His tires squealed as we drove away into the night.

"Where to?" Erik asked.

"To Ryparken House in Fredens Park, on Norrebro Street. Hurry, I'm late for the Danish Resistance meeting. I won't be long and I will take Johna with me. Pick us up there in an hour," said Far.

"I'll come in and find you, if you are late. Be careful," Erik said. He stopped a few yards from Fredens Park and let us out of the car, then slowly drove off.

Far took my hand and we walked into the dim shadows of the park toward the outline of a house. The cold wind and rain came in gusts, soaking my hair and clothes. Suddenly a loud bang came from within the park, startling me.

Far dragged me behind a bush and put his hand gently over my mouth.

My heart pounding, I peeked from behind the bush. Across the way from where we hid, German soldiers were tying three men to fence posts. After they were done, the soldiers dipped handkerchiefs in the water puddles and slapped them on the men's chests. The men tied to the posts all screamed something, but it was drowned out by the laughter of the soldiers. As I watched this strange scene, one of the officers lifted his pistol and fired shots through the center of each one of those handkerchiefs. Blood gushed from the men as they doubled up and slumped away from the cords that held them to the posts.

Just then, Far jerked me upright. He swept me up into his arms and began to run out of the park, keeping low behind the bushes. He rushed into a nearby apartment foyer and we hid behind a staircase. Then I heard a sob. I looked up and Far was crying. This frightened me so much I began to cry, too.

I wondered what had happened. Who were the men tied to the fence? What had happened to them? Of course, they had been killed, but at that time, none of these things had much meaning for me. All I knew was that Far, who always told me only babies cried, was crying because of what had happened. I clung to him in terror.

We stayed in the foyer holding onto each other until Erik somehow found us. He guided us out to the street where we climbed into the safety of his car. Far told him how we had hidden in the bushes, and what we had seen from there.

"My God, this is so terrible Poul! It's an evil atrocity, a witch-hunt, killing Danish citizens without a trial. I want to kill all those son of bitches! I heard on the streets about the shootings. Most of your comrades at the resistance meeting are dead. Some few got away, though, and they told me that you were not there yet when the Gestapo came. I drove around looking for you. God damn them," he said, hitting the steering wheel with the palm of his hand.

"God damn them!"

"Those Nazi swine put handkerchiefs over their hearts as a

target. Can you believe that?" said Far, his voice was rough, and broke when he spoke.

We pulled up in front of our apartment building and Far opened the door to get out.

"Here is a bottle of whiskey, Poul," said Erik, handing him a bottle. "Just drink yourself to sleep. I'll see you tomorrow, all right?" Far took the bottle and nodded.

That night, Far let me sleep with him all night.

Chapter 16

The Wagon Man

The next morning Far rolled over, gave me a kiss, and got out of bed. I covered my head with the feather comforter, not wanting to get out of the soft bed.

"Johna, get up, we're going to visit Mor today."

I popped up from under the covers. "I'm not tired anymore, Far!"

"I thought not!" he said, smiling at me. He laid out my green and white polka-dot dress, white socks and shoes. I wondered why he wouldn't let me choose my own clothes to go see Mor, but I didn't ask. I was just glad to be going. After a breakfast of bread with only butter on it and raw oatmeal and sugar mixed in a bowl, Far combed my hair, pulling out snags.

"Come now, let's go," said Far, hurrying me toward the door. I started to run, but Far grabbed my hand.

"Slow down, Johna. Stay by me and hold on tight to my hand, I don't want you to blow away. Besides if you're running all around you'll attract the attention of the Germans." I slowed down, bowed my head down as Mor had taught me to do, and watched my shoes click on the cobbled street.

We were first in line for the streetcar, but as our trolley came to a stop, Far motioned for the German soldier who had come up behind us to move to the front. We ended up across the aisle from the soldier. It made my hands shake to see him so close, so I just looked out the trolley window and pretended he wasn't there.

The hospital grounds still had pretty flowers blooming, even though it was late in the season. Tall trees lined the sidewalk. Entering the hospital doors, I gripped Far's callused hand as we strolled down the long hallway. When I passed each open door I tried to look into each of the rooms to see if Mor were there. People in the corridor stared at us as we passed.

"Far, it stinks in here!" I said. "It smells like mothballs and icky medicine."

"I know. Now hush, Johna," he whispered to me and pried my hand from his. Far tapped me on top of my head, reminding me to be quiet.

A nurse dressed in a white uniform that swished as she walked came to meet us. She took us through a green glass door to an almost empty room. A few metal chairs lined the walls. The windows were covered by wire. Mor, in a white linen robe and with no makeup on, sat in a wheelchair waiting for us.

"Mor! Mor!" My cries echoed off the walls. I jumped up on her lap. She hugged and kissed me, but squirmed as if I was hurting her. Far bent down to Mor and gave her a kiss on the cheek.

"Can you come home now?" I asked.

"Not yet, but it won't be too long and I will come home, Little Skat," she said.

"How long is not too long?"

"Damn!" Far said. "She always comes out with questions. Other kids her age don't question everything. Where does she get this chatting from? It is very annoying. She is to be seen, not heard. I just know it is not normal."

"Poul, she's just a bright child, her teacher tells me she is gifted, and has her own mind."

"What?! She is just an ordinary child with an imagination."

"What happened to your face, Poul?" said Mor, changing the subject.

"Oh, I slipped and fell at work," Far lied. "I'm just fine. You look awful, Margit," he said, changing the subject in his turn. "Are you all right?"

"No! They've put me in this mental ward. I don't like it. One woman rocks back and forth on the floor all day, whimpering scary sounds. Another one stands by the window and talks to people who aren't there. She pees herself and smells awful. And there is a crazy woman who walks in her sleep—she wakes me up to see fireworks that aren't there. Please get me out of here Poul, please?" Mor pleaded.

"Calm down, Margit. Just calm down. I'm trying to get you out of here safely. I'll do all I can for you," Far reassured her. Then he asked a funny question.

"Has the doctor taken the baby?"

"*Ja*, yesterday," said Mor, looking down for a minute. Then she looked back up at Far.

"Have you visited my parents?" she asked, but immediately started to cry. I hugged her, not understanding her tears.

"I'm not forgetting them, Margit. I promised you I'd take care of them, and I will. They are safe and doing just fine." Far lit his pipe and held the match up to my face to blow out the flame. "Most of the Jews are hiding. It's safer for you to stay here a bit longer."

"Oh, Poul, is it really that bad?"

"Yes. The Germans are becoming crueler and even killed a few Danes that got in their way when the soldiers were rounding up the Jews. Even Arne's dog, Bueller, was cut."

"They would hurt a dog? How did that happen?" Mor asked.

"Arne and I were just walking Bueller on a leash, but the dog kept barking at two German soldiers ahead of us. They turned around and faced us. One of them took out his knife, and sliced the dog from his tail to his neck. I was so angry I wanted to kill him, but he had a knife and a rifle, and all I had was my fist. Arne told me not to do something foolish. Blood was gushing out on Bueller's white fur making it look pink."

"Oh, my God! Is he dead?"

"No, we rushed him to the vet, and he sewed him up."

I had not heard this news about Bueller, who was a favorite of mine. "Was Bueller really bleeding real blood Far?" I sobbed, "like the men on the poles in the park?" Mor held me tighter and brushed my hair back from my forehead.

"Poul, you are scaring Johna and me. What is happening to our peaceful country? And what is Johna talking about? What men? What has she seen? Are you not protecting her?" Mor said in anger.

Far bent down and kissed me and ruffled his hands through my curly hair.

"Margit, be brave. Trust me, I am taking care of Johna. I plan for all of us to get out of Copenhagen to a safer place."

"My parents, too?"

"*Ja*, of course your parents. I said *all* of us."

"Oh, oy, what an awful time this is," Mor said as I turned her head with my hand for her to look at me.

"Did Mr. Larsen's pigeon give you my note?" I asked her. She looked at Far, who nodded his head.

"Yes, Johna, that was nice," she said, and gave me a thin smile.

Far kept looking at his watch.

"Come, Johna," he said. "Erik is going to pick us up. We've got to go, and Mor needs some rest." Far opened the door to the hallway and motioned to the nurse that we were through with our visit.

Erik, dressed up as usual in his suit and tie, stood waiting for us by his black car. We all got in and he drove us over to Farmor's.

When we got there, I saw the neon sign on the Café Absolan was off. I had never seen it off before. A card stuck in the window said "CLOSED." We walked toward the café. A man with no legs, whom I called the "Wagon Man," pushed his wooden-wheeled platform with his hands along the sidewalk until he blocked the entrance of the café. He wore a red knitted hat and dirty clothes. I had seen him many times at Farmor's. He would come to the back kitchen door of the café and Farmor's cooks would give him left over scraps of food.

"Can you spare some coins for me today, Poul?" the wagon man asked.

"No!" said Far. "Fuck off and move out of the way."

"You think you are such a big man!" the wagon man said, "but your little girl is a Jew!"

"Who would like to know that, I wonder? All you have to do is give me a few coins and I won't tell the Germans anything."

"God damn you! You are a heartless swine bastard. I'll pull you off that cart and bash your head in!" Erik said.

"I'm not afraid of you," the wagon man sneered.

"You should be, you piece of shit!" Far's face flashed with anger. Without looking at me, he said, "Johna, walk around him and go into the café."

I did as Far said, happy to get away from the wagon man. I opened the entrance door and closed it behind me. I peeked out of a small diamond window in the door panel. I saw Far with his hand over the little man's mouth. Then Erik lifted the wagon man out of his wagon and carried him, struggling, into the alley.

I turned around and saw some people sitting at a table in the café with just a candle for light. I ran by them to the kitchen, where Farmor stood alone, wiping her hands with a towel. She clasped her big arms around me, picked me up, and squeezed me into her large, soft breasts.

"Where's Far?" she asked.

"Outside with Erik and the man in the wagon," I said.

"Oh!" Farmor said, and looked toward the door of the café.

Just then the kitchen door opened. Far propped the door open with his shoe for Erik, who came in behind him. Both Erik's and Far's shirts were covered with blood, and their hand were bruised and bloody. They took their shirts off and dumped them in the garbage can in the corner.

"Oh, my goodness," Farmor groaned. "What has happened?"

I stared at the two of them in terror. More blood, I thought, looking at their bruised hands. What did it mean this time? They went to the sink. I watched them grimacing in pain as they washed the blood from their hands and faces. Then with another wet rag, they cleaned the blood from their pants. Farmor pulled two jackets from hooks behind the kitchen door and handed them to Far and Erik.

Erik saw me and came over and picked me up. With Far and Farmor following, he carried me into the tavern. At a big table with just one candle giving it light, sat Uncle Arne, Uncle Orla, Alfred, Myra, mean Carl, and some others I didn't know.

"Johna, I don't want you to say a word, no talking. Just sit and be still," Far whispered in my ear. "Do you hear me?" He pinched my arm and looked hard at me, which meant I was to do as he said. I touched where he had pinched me and wondered what I had done wrong. I was now so afraid of everything.

Hardly anyone spoke at the table, and I was too scared to say anything even if I had wanted to. We soon left and walked up the staircase to an empty room. Inside, guns and money lay on the bed.

"Carl, would you go with my mother and Johna and help bring us some food and beer?" Far asked. Carl came over and grabbed my hand to pull me with him. I screamed and tried to get away from him, looking at Farmor for help.

"Let go of Johna!" Farmor said to him. He did and I ran

to her. She put her arm around me, and then she and I walked down to the kitchen together. Once there, Carl opened the beer cupboards and got the beer, while Farmor sliced salami, bread, and cheese, then buttered the bread.

"What's that noise?" said Farmor, looking around at a scratching noise. "Oh, it's that damn cat behind the stove again."

"I'll get it, Farmor," I said. "I'll put the cat outside."

"Good, Johna...that cat likes you and will come to you."

I cornered the big black cat between the stove and the wall. He came right to me, purring. He was so huge his back half hung below my arms when I picked him up. I backed out the kitchen door and stepped onto the rear landing. I put the cat down and it scurried down the concrete steps. I looked around to my left and saw a dark lump in the corner of the alley. A small pool of blood and a red knitted cap lay in the shadows next to it.

"Farmor! Farmor!" I yelled, "There's blood and something strange lying in the alley!" Farmor rushed out the kitchen door and looked where I pointed. Then she scooped me into her arms again. Holding me tight, she said, "Don't look, Little Skat. I will see to it later. Don't look."

She carried me back into the kitchen and closed the door behind her. She held me tight for a bit more, then set me down and looked into my face.

"You must forget what you have seen, all right? It's nothing. It is just blood from the butchered beef I hang out in the alley to keep cool. It must have looked scary in the dark," she said, hugging me again, "but it's nothing to be afraid of." Motioning me to follow, she picked up the tray of sandwiches and we headed back up the stairs. When we entered the bedroom again, the guns and money were not on the bed anymore.

I stayed with Farmor that night. I don't know where Far and Erik went. All night, all I could see was the color of red. Whenever I closed my eyes, I saw the red, knitted cap lying on the ground in the alley. I thought of Bueller the dog with his fur pink with blood. I saw men with handkerchiefs on their chests spreading red, and pictured a beef carcass dripping blood into a pool on the ground. Terrified by these pictures, I tried to keep my eyes open until Farmor got under the covers with me.

Chapter 17

Sudden Departure

Far came early the next morning to pick me up. I was waiting for him in the café, but I was sweating with a fever and had a cough.

"What's the matter with Johna," he asked Farmor. "Is she sick? She is hacking and coughing."

"She has a fever. She's not well, Son." As Farmor answered, my stomach suddenly began to roll like I was seasick. I ran as fast as I could to the kitchen where I gagged and threw up into the sink on top of all the dirty dishes.

"Far, I couldn't make it to the bathroom toilet in the hall. Are you mad at me?" I asked.

"No, I'm not mad at you," he said. Then he turned to Farmor. "I'm picking up Margit from the hospital today. It is getting too dangerous to keep her there any longer. The Germans are now checking the hospital wards for Jews. Will you please go pick up Emma, Alfred's girlfriend, from the hospital and bring her here? She'll stay with you until I can get her out of Denmark. Emma knows you are coming for her."

"I'll go get her right away," said Farmor. "Let me take care of Johna until she gets well."

"No," said Far, "I'll take Johna home and put her to bed. I know how to take care of a sick child, Mother. Besides, Margit is coming home late this evening, and I know she'll want to see her."

"Mor is coming home?" I said, hardly able to believe what I had heard.

"That's right, Johna," said Far, laughing at me. "You heard right. Mor is coming home." Far took me outside and whistled for a taxi. It wasn't long after that that I was snuggled in my own bed with some hot lemon tea on the bedside table.

"I need to leave, Johna," Far said. "You'll be fine for a bit by yourself, won't you? I think you just have your mother's nervous stomach, nothing else. Mor will be here in a few hours, and until then, Mrs. Johnsen from upstairs will come down and check on you."

I started to get up and protest, but Far cut me off.

"Now, don't fret," he said, pushing me gently back into the bed, "you won't have to go into her hidden closet."

That was good news, but best would have been if I could have gone with him. It made me uneasy to think of him leaving me behind. In a few minutes, though, Mrs. Johnsen arrived. Then Far kissed my hot forehead and headed toward the door.

"Don't worry, Poul, Johna will be fine," Mrs. Johnsen assured him.

As I saw Far go out the door, terror swept through me and I began to sob. I was so afraid he wouldn't come back. With Mor gone, he was all I had left of my world. Mrs. Johnsen reached over and took me in her arms and comforted me. I tried to think of Mor coming home, and how happy I would be when she did, and slowly my sobs quieted down.

"There, there, Johna, that's better," said Mrs. Johnsen, rocking me back and forth. "Your father thinks you should stay in bed, but today is Friday, my clothes washing day. The steam in the wash room might help what ails you."

The minute she said that it made me think of Mr. Larsen's beautiful, soft birds.

"May I go up and see the pigeons?" I asked.

"It will be locked, but I'm sure Mr. Larsen won't mind if you peeked in on them."

I climbed out of bed and soon we headed up to the laundry room together. While Mrs. Johnsen attended to the clothes, I went over to the ladder to the pigeon platform. After climbing all the stairs to the laundry room, I felt shaky on my feet as I went up the ladder, just like when Far gave me whiskey to drink to go to sleep.

I was part way up when I realized I couldn't hear any cooing. That seemed strange to me. Then, as I got closer to their cages, I smelled something awful. I looked in and saw all the birds lying still on the bottom of their cages.

"Mrs. Johnsen! Mrs. Johnsen!" I yelled. "The pigeons are sick, too. They are all lying down on their sides!" She hurried up to the platform and looked over my shoulder at the pigeon cages. Then, without saying a word, she grabbed me by the hand and hurried me down the back stairs from the loft to Mr. Larsen's apartment, where she banged her fist on his door. He opened the door in his underwear, and stood there rubbing his eyes with the palms of his hands.

"I was taking a nap. What do you want?"

"Something terrible is wrong with your birds," said Mrs. Johnsen.

Without even stopping to put on his pants, Mr. Larsen pushed by us and ran up the stairs.

"What is wrong with the pigeons?" I asked Mrs. Johnsen.

"Don't you worry, Johna, Mr. Larsen will look after his birds. They will be fine, I'm sure.

I'll take you back to your bed now," said Mrs. Johnsen, and she led me back to my own apartment.

She tucked me into my bed and I lay there, cuddled up to my comforter, and waited for Mor. The day passed slowly, and I drifted in and out of sleep. Late in the day the front door opened and I heard Mrs. Johnsen say, "Margit! You're home!"

I held my breath and listened. Did she say Margit? Mrs. Johnsen said something else, but I couldn't understand the words. Then someone else spoke back.

"Johna is ill?" the voice said. It was the magical sound of Mor's voice.

"Mor!" I shrieked, and jumped out of bed and ran into the hall. We hugged and kissed. I was so happy. I knew that now my life would be back to normal. I would be able to go and play with Hanne and my friends again, and maybe even go to school again. I clung to Mor, afraid to let go of her for even a minute.

Mrs. Johnsen and Mor spoke for a few moments, then Mrs. Johnsen sat down on the couch. Mor fixed me some white powdered medicine in a glass of honey tea, wrapped me up in a blanket, and sat with me on her lap in Far's chair. It felt so good to have her back again and feel her close to me.

Mrs. Johnsen was telling her how the Germans had searched our building looking for Jews when Mr. Larsen walked in our door, dressed now, and followed by Far.

"My pigeons—it's poison—just the sort of thing the Germans would do," Mr. Larsen said.

"Wonder how they did it?" asked Far. "The Germans are not smart enough to narrow anything down to particulars."

"An enemy among us, perhaps?...we will never know," said Mr. Larsen, shaking his head back and forth, his eyes filling with tears.

"I'm so sorry about your birds," said Mrs. Johnsen, "but I must go finish my wash." With that she headed for the door. Mr. Larsen stared blankly after her.

"Let's you and I go see about this," said Far, and motioned to Mr. Larsen to follow him.

The two of them then headed up the stairs to the loft.

"Will the pigeons get medicine and be well again, Mor?" I asked.

"Yes, Little Skat," said Mor, "but now it's time for you to rest in your bed so you can get better."

I crawled into my bed, and with Mor home again at last, soon fell fast asleep.

The next morning when I woke, Far had already left.

"Johna, you look better today," said Mor when she came in to feel my forehead.

"I'm not sick any longer, Mor."

"Good, I'm taking a quick shower, then I'll fix breakfast. Far will be home soon to eat with us."

I sat in the hallway outside the bathroom and played with my doll. Suddenly, I heard the sound of heavy boots coming up on the stairwell, followed by pounding of something hard against the door.

"Open up!" a loud voice cried.

I ran to the window in the living room that faced the street and peeked through the closed drapes. Germans were all over the street. I didn't know what to do and wondered if I should hide in the chest as Far had had me do before. I didn't, though. Instead I opened the bathroom door and whispered, "Mor, I think there are German soldiers at the door."

Mor pulled me into the running shower, then reached over and gently locked the bathroom door.

"Shh," she said to me, and held onto me. We stood, trembling in the shower, until the hot water ran out.

"I'm cold, Mor," I whispered, my teeth chattering. Mor turned off the shower then, and helped me take off my wet clothes. We tiptoed into the living room and peeked again through the drapes. We saw no Germans outside. The street was silent.

"Can I talk now?" I asked.

"Yes, they are gone," said Mor, putting the back of her hand to her forehead. After we both got dressed, we went to the kitchen to boil some water for our morning oatmeal.

"Mor," I said, going back into the living room, "I know how to hide in the chest." I wasn't sure if she had heard me, but I slipped inside the chest and waited.

"Oj! Oj! Johna, where are you? Oh, my God! Johna! Johna!" Mor called out. I could tell she was upset.

"Mor! I'm in here!" I said, and peaked out from under the heavy lid of the chest.

"Johna, don't you ever do that again, do you hear me?"

Far came in the door just as she said that.

"What's wrong, Margit?" he asked. She told him of the Germans knocking on our door, being in the shower, and the scare I had given her by hiding in the chest.

"Good girl!" said Far, looking at me. He turned back to Mor. "She is just doing what I told her to do, Margit. I told her to hide there if anyone came to the door. By the way, I just came from seeing your parents. They are fine. Your papa complains of nothing to read, being cooped up in that 'gentile cage of a house.' He's afraid to play his violin, because all he knows is Hebrew music. Your mother just prays."

"Poor Papa. Can you arrange for me to see them, Poul?"

"No, not now. But you will be reunited soon. I have made arrangements to hide your parents' valuables and a few things of ours. With the help of a friend I have deposited them in a Swiss bank. The accounts will be under my name and your father's name of Pressmann. We can collect it later when this damn war is over."

"My God! My parents are in their seventies and not so young anymore, will they live through this?" asked Mor.

"Not without my help," said Far. "Your father is a stubborn Jew, but he will have to do what I tell him or he will die."

"With God's help we can all get out of this nightmare," said Mor, closing her eyes tight.

"Look around you, Margit, do you see God anywhere?" said Far, his words angry and hard. "Oh, yes, he's here! But he's in German uniforms with swastikas on the arms. I have news for you, the Germans think they are God! They push us around, but I will not allow them to do that to me!" said Far, his eyes piercing.

"Stop it, Poul!" Mor shouted at him.

"*Ja, Ja*...just pack some clothes for us and I will be back soon. Be ready to leave when I get here. We'll go to my mother's and stay there for a little while. The Germans who drink downstairs in the tavern would not suspect her of knowing any Jews. We will decide what to do and when to leave for Sweden." Far closed the door and left.

Mor packed our clothes and family photos into our suitcases.

"Johna, we are going to Farmor's, and there the bad Germans won't scare us."

"All Germans are not bad. Alfred is Far's friend," I said.

"Alfred? Who is he? Where did you meet a German soldier?"

"Oh, Mor, it is a secret!" I said.

"Tell me, Johna!...You can tell me."

"I met him and other Germans," I hesitated, then continued, "when I was with Farmor, while you were in the hospital."

"Who were the others?"

"Just Germans. They drink beer." I didn't tell her about Myra and mean Carl.

"You keep a secret well, Johna," Mor said, looking at me closely. But she didn't know how much I knew, and I was suddenly afraid I might slip up and let more secrets out. When Far arrived we had no time for more breakfast than just a bite of bread and butter. We swallowed it down quickly, then Far grabbed the packed suitcases and we hurried down the street to a waiting taxi. I had managed to grab my doll, Jette, and wrapped her in her blanket as we drove to Farmor's.

When we got to Farmor's, Mor and I started getting out of the cab, but Far stayed in.

"Margit," he said through the window, "I'm not coming in with you, but I will be back to eat dinner."

Mor and I watched the taxi drive away with Far still inside, and then we walked down the alley to the door that led upstairs to Farmor's apartment above the café. I thought about the blood—and the red knitted cap in the alley—and stopped walking. I didn't want to go any further. Mor jerked on my hand, turning me away from the alley to climb up the stairwell to Farmor's apartment. It smelled of cat pee.

When we got to the top of the stairs, a man was sitting on a chair in front of Farmor's door. He greeted us with a smile and opened the locked door. When we walked in, Farmor and her maid, Marie, hugged us. We all went in and sat on the living room sofa. A woman was already sitting there on one of the cushions. Mor's eyes opened wide, and she put down her suitcase with a thud.

"Margit, I think you know Emma," Farmor said.

"I saw her at your café a long time ago, but I don't know her," said Mor, and her voice was not so friendly.

"My Jewish family were taken away by the Germans and I am so grateful to your husband and to Alfred," Emma started to say.

"Who is Alfred? I have heard that name before," Mor said.

Farmor rose from the sofa and said, "No need for you to know. Don't ask questions, Margit."

Mor looked at Farmor for a moment and then just sat down on the bed without saying another word.

We spent the rest of the day in Farmor's apartment. Marie played with me while the others did the cooking and baking in the kitchen. She read me stories and drew funny looking cartoons that made me laugh.

Farmor came in at one point and said, "If you have to go pee tell me and I will take you to the bathroom out in the hallway by the front door."

"Ja, Farmor...Farmor? Why is a man sitting in a chair by your door?" I asked.

"He protects us from bad Germans."

"Do only nice Germans come to eat and drink beer downstairs?"

"Sure, just the nice ones," said Farmor, but once again I wondered how one could tell if a German is bad or nice.

The odor of the pork roast and the sweet smell of the red cabbage made me hungry.

Following the smell, I went to see what was happening in the kitchen. Mor had her back to me, but turned when she heard me come in. When she did, I stared at her hands—they were stained purple from preparing pickled beets for the salad.

Just then, heavy footsteps pounded up the stairs and Far, out of breath, appeared in the doorway.

"Hurry!" he said. "Let's go...now!"

Mor stared at him in surprise for a moment, and then rushed me into the bedroom and opened her suitcase.

"Johna, here, put on some more clothes, as you do for the air raid shelter."

"Are the Germans coming?"

"Shh, do as I told you!" Mor snapped.

"Hurry, let's get moving!" said Far and paced the floor, stopping every little bit to star out the window. Then he turned and winked at Emma.

"We will be going to a dairy farm near the sea on the outskirts of Elisnor. Friends will be there. The secret code is 'Elisnor Sewing Club,'" Far said to Mor.

"Poul, why is Emma here, and who is Alfred?...and what about my parents, did you go and get them?"

"They are waiting for us in Erik's car. I'll tell you later about Emma. Now, let's go" he urged.

Mor put my blue coat on me. It barely fit over the extra layers of clothing that I had on. It was uncomfortable and I didn't like it. I didn't like any of it. Far's sudden urgency frightened me and I didn't want to leave Farmor's.

"Mor, we have to eat first. I'm hungry," I whined.

"Never mind, Johna," she answered.

"But Mor," I said, "your hands are stained purple. Aren't you going to wash them? We can't go—you should clean your hands off. Mor! I'm hungry," I babbled on and on.

"The child has to eat something," said Farmor. "I will fix some sandwiches to take with you."

"There is no time, Mother!" said Far. "We're leaving right now. Germans are rounding up Jews everywhere. Someone painted "Jude" on our apartment door. Don't you understand? There are no safe places and there's no time left. Let's go!" Far pushed Mor and I toward the door.

"Mor, wash your hands!" I shouted again, now terrified by the beet juice on them.

"Quiet, Johna! Shut up now!" said Far, his tone sharp. I looked up at him and closed my mouth, as frightened of him as I was of leaving.

Farmor and Marie were both crying as they hugged us, and told us good-bye. Everything in me hurt. I tried to hang on to Farmor, but couldn't because Far was moving us out. Suddenly he stopped and turned to Mor.

"Margit, give your fur coat to Marie," he said, and began to pull the mink off Mor.

"No, Poul!" said Mor, pulling away from him. "I don't want to leave it!"

"It stays, Margit. They can sell it and send money to us," said Far. "Life has changed, Margit. Who knows how quickly I'll find work in Sweden, or even if we'll be able to stay in Sweden. Any bit of money we can get will be needed."

He took Mor's beautiful mink and handed it to Marie, taking her warm, black wool coat in exchange and handing it to Mor to put on. Mor did so without looking up. Then Far took me by the hand and we ran down the stairwell, shooing the cats ahead of us out into the alleyway courtyard.

Far pushed me headfirst into the back seat of Erik's car. To my delight Zayde and Bubbe were already there. I crawled up on Zayde's lap and my feet clanked on his violin case on the floor of the car. Mor, Far, and Emma squeezed into the front seat. As Erik drove off, Zayde moved to the middle so I could sit by the window.

"I'm hot and I'm hungry," I said, and Bubbe reached over and helped me remove my coat.

"Shut up, Johna," Far hushed me.

"Shh," Zayde said, looking at my sad face.

I sat quiet, looking out the window. I tried to focus on

the trees that lined the dark road away from Farmor's. I felt captive, dizzy, almost in a trance as I watched them stream by. I suddenly knew we were not going home again and the thought made me tremble.

"Ohhhh," I whimpered and began to cry.

Far reached over the back of the front seat and lifted me up on his lap. I buried my face in his shoulder not wanting to look out the window anymore. All I saw were things going away from me. I remained there, not moving, until the car slowed and stopped. Erik turned off the dim, blue, blackout lights that glowed from the headlights. We all got out and, with Erik and Far leading the way with flashlights, we left the car and entered the darkness of a forest.

Chapter 18

Escape

It was black once we were under the trees and I couldn't see my way through the twists and turns on a path that didn't seem to lead anywhere but deeper into the forest. We stumbled over sticks and roots on the forest floor, breaking the stillness of the night, with only the sound of our shoes scuffling through the fall leaves.

Mor's icy hand clutched mine too hard as she held me to the path. Those ahead of us had turned to shadows, appearing and disappearing in the dim flashlight beams as Erik and Far led us further into the woods.

"Mor, it's spooky...I can't see anything. Where are we going?" I whined, forgetting to be quiet.

"SHH!" I heard from somewhere in the woods. Startled, we all stopped short. My heart pounded. Far pointed the beam of his flashlight toward where the sound had come from. The light landed on many men, women, and children where they sat huddled quietly in the dark, their white faces reflecting the light from the flashlight.

Behind us, a sudden scream from Zayde broke the silence. We heard the sound of falling rocks, a thump, a crunch, and then silence again.

Far's flashlight clicked off, leaving only darkness. I heard the sound of footsteps coming toward and then past me. My eyes adjusted to the darkness, but even so, I couldn't see where Far had gone. The flashlights came on again a little away from us and began to move toward us. Far and Erik, one on each side of Zayde, were helping him up from the hole where he had fallen. He was hopping on one foot.

"My violin, oy!" said Zayde, and tried to turn to go back where he had fallen.

"NO!" said Far. "We can't go back for it...besides it's broken."

"SHH!" The people in the dark said again.

Far helped Zayde with his twisted ankle over to where Mor and I were. He told us to sit down under a large tree.

"We shall return as soon as we can," he whispered, then he and Erik left us. I could hear the sound of twigs breaking beneath their steps and followed the beams of their flashlights until they, too, disappeared into the night.

"Why are we here in the dark?" I asked Mor softly.

"We're playing a game so the Germans can't find us," Mor whispered back. "Now, Johna, you must be quiet, or I'll have to put tape over your mouth."

"But, Mor," I whispered, "I have to go to the bathroom."

Mor took me a few steps away from the tree and the other people, and we peed in the dark, without even wiping with toilet paper. I still wanted to ask what we were waiting for, but I didn't dare. Mor had said this was a game, but nothing about it was fun and it made me afraid.

"Take a nap, Little Skat, it will be a long time before Far and Erik return," Mor whispered to me, and sat me down on the suitcase. But I couldn't get comfortable on it, so I sat on the damp ground. My teeth chattered from the cold and damp and my stomach gnawed with hunger. I was miserable, and felt greatly sorry for myself. Mor began to sing quietly in my ear to calm me. She chose a song about a red umbrella, and I couldn't help but listen.

> *Little Ole with the red umbrella*
> *He sees all small children in the town*
> *Every little girl*
> *Every little boy*
> *That sleeps sweetly*
> *In their little beds*

The sound of her soft voice calmed me, but the night was long and sleep only came in spurts. And each time I did sleep, bad dreams of me standing in the beams of German flashlights woke me again.

Finally the sky began to lighten. Just before the sun came

up a man passed out water in a flask, along with some raw turnips dug from a nearby farmer's field. I didn't like the taste of raw turnips and spit them out.

"Mor, can I talk a little bit?" I whispered, tugging on her arm.

"Yes, Johna. What is it?"

"Where is Far, will he be here soon?"

"Far will be here when it gets dark again," said Mor.

It seemed as if she were angry, so I did not ask anything more. Instead, I looked around in the light at the other people sitting out in the woods with us.

The grownups were all wrapped in black coats, and the women wore black scarves on their heads. One old man held a tin box and sat amongst many suitcases, cardboard boxes, and brown paper bundles tied with string. A young boy had caught a brown bunny and lay in the dirt petting it. The other children stared at me, but said nothing. Mothers with babies breast-fed them to keep them quiet.

The time passed so slowly. For a long while I lay in Zayde's arms. At one point a scuffle broke out when a man tried to light his pipe. Two other men close to him took it away from him. When the scuffle broke out, I asked Zayde why those men would not let the man smoke.

"Because," he whispered back, "the Germans might smell the smoke or see the flame. Now, you must be still, Johna. Please."

This sitting still was so hard. After a bit, I moved away from where Zayde, Bubbe, and Emma sat together, and crawled back to where Mor sat across from them.

"Mor, Emma is pretty," I said.

"Have you seen Far with Emma?" Mor asked me.

"No," I answered, glad that she did not ask about Myra.

I crawled back over to Bubbe and Zayde, seeking protection and the warmth of their bodies. I was careful not to bump Zayde's twisted ankle or he would push me back to Mor. Soon the late autumn sun filtered through the trees, warming the patches of ground where it landed. The warmth made sleep come easier and after the long, wakeful night, I slept through most of the day, waking only in spurts to complain of my hunger. When the sun went down, the cold returned.

Sometime after it was completely dark, two lights flickered toward us through the trees.

"Margit, where are you?" Far whispered in a hoarse voice. "Come on, we're leaving."

We all stood up and moved toward Far, carrying our bundles. Erik came forward to help Zayde, who still couldn't walk on his ankle. Moving carefully through the dark, we made our way out of the forest and onto the road where an ambulance waited. When I saw the ambulance there, I became afraid that Mor might be going away again. I clung to her as hard as I could when she started to climb in, but then, to my relief, she pulled me in with her.

About twenty people squeezed into the back of the ambulance with us. Far climbed in last and pulled the doors shut behind him, enclosing us in near darkness. Mor held me tight, and Far sat next to me by the door. The ambulance started up and began to move down the road. A small panel separated the back from the front of the ambulance. After we had been driving a short while, it slid open and Erik poked his head through.

"There's a German roadblock ahead," he told everyone in the back. "Don't panic, and don't make a sound." Then he closed the panel again.

The people around us all bowed their heads and looked down at their feet. Far stood up and pulled a small pillow from a rack above my head.

"Johna, I will be setting this pillow on your lap. I want you to put your face in the pillow so you won't look. I'll hold the back of your head with my hand to keep you down." Far took off my glasses. I didn't want to put my face in the pillow and flung my arms around in protest, but he shoved my head into the pillow before I could say anything. My whole body was shaking.

"Poul, why are you doing that?" said Mor. "Can't you see she is frightened?"

"If they shoot us, I don't want Johna to see," Far said.

I lifted my face from the small pillow.

"Someone is going to shoot me?" I asked.

Far pushed my head into the pillow again, and whispered, "Little Skat, if you do what I tell you, no one will be shot. If you do *exactly* as I tell you, I will buy you a red umbrella like you wanted, like the one Hanne has."

The promise of a red umbrella suddenly turned this into a much easier thing to do and I gave in. I scooted closer to Mor and put my head into the pillow. Mor was shaking just like me. Suddenly, I heard the ambulance doors open with a loud clang, followed by a rifle shot. I felt a rush of cold air, then heard laughter. Far's hand pressed my face harder into the pillow. Red and yellow lights flashed behind my eyes. After some minutes, Far lifted his hand from my head and I came up gasping for air, tears streaming down my face. The ambulance doors slammed closed again, shutting us up in the dim space once again. Mor gathered me into her arms and wiped both our tears away with her hand. I looked up at Far.

"You're my brave girl," he said, and smiled at me.

"Can I have the red umbrella?" I asked. My fear had not made me forget the promise of that umbrella.

"Ja," Far answered, chuckling. "Ja."

"Poul, why didn't they kill us?" Mor asked. Before Far could answer her, Erik's blond head appeared through the opening in the panel again.

"A Danish Nazi outside told us they know we are trying to hide Jews from them. They say they will get more Jews if they wait until later. They say they will find us."

"Oy, God, Poul," Mor said, looking at Far, her eyes wide with fear.

"No, Margit they just think they know. Other resistance fighters are taking care of that, I hope. It was our plan in case we got stopped," Far said.

The ambulance started to move again.

"Mor, I heard a gunshot. Who got shot? Is there blood on anyone?" I asked, remembering the men in the park.

"What? How do you know to ask such a question?"

"I don't know," I lied, not wanting to tell her about how Far and I had hidden behind the bushes and watched the Germans tie Far's friends to stakes and shoot them. I was sure that this was a secret I had to keep. "Was it the bad Germans?" I asked to change the subject.

"No, they did not hurt us did they? They were shooting up in the sky, hunting birds," Mor said.

"Oh," I said, wondering if the Germans would hunt and shoot a stork.

The ambulance finally came to a stop, and we got out. We stood on a dirt road and clouds covered the moon.

"I have to go pick up twenty more people from the woods," said Erik, and he climbed back in the ambulance and drove away.

Just then the full moon broke through the overcast and lit a path through a field that led us to a farm. Cows gathered along the barbed wire fence and stared at us. A few stretched their heads through the fence to smell us. We all filed along the fence at the edge of the field until we came to the U-shaped farmstead ahead of us. A glow of lights flickered from behind the curtained windows of the house that was connected to the barn. A farmer in overalls and rubber boots held a kerosene lantern and directed us across the yard into the open door of the cow barn. Inside, the cow stalls were empty, but the gutters smelled of fresh cow poop. The farmer held the lantern high and motioned us toward a ladder that went from the floor of the barn to the loft above.

"Climb up to the loft and make room for others," said the farmer. "And keep silent."

Far had put a black armband on his upper arm. I asked Mor what that meant and she said it showed that he was a 'helper,' though I didn't know what that meant. Far waved us all toward the ladder. It was hard for some of the older people to climb, so people below them boosted them up with their shoulders. Then the person would stretch their arms and pull themselves up to the next rung of the ladder. Between their pulling and the pushing from those below them, they eventually pulled themselves up into the loft.

Mor and I didn't need any help, but Zayde did. First Far wrapped his ankle tight with his neck scarf to protect it, but even so, Zayde cried out in pain as Far and another man struggled to push him up the ladder.

Once up in the loft the only light we had was the moon shining through the cracks of the wood and that which came through from a large opening in the upper wall. It was enough, however, for me to recognize other people were already huddled on the hayloft floor.

"Mor, is this a Jewish barn?"

"Yes, I guess it is," said Mor as we sat down on the hay piled on the slick wood floor of the loft.

Once again there was nothing to do but sit in the dark. I could hear mice running around underneath the hay and it scared me. Around me, people coughed, some of the babies fussed, and constant murmuring filled the night.

My stomach was hungry and my head started to itch. I scratched at it, and said," I want to eat."

"Johna, just be still and God will stop your hunger," Zayde whispered.

"How?"

"There is a time for everything and now is not a time to eat. Tonight we must fast to cleanse our bodies," said Zayde.

"I'm not going to eat?" I asked, but Zayde had no answer for me. Instead, Mor gave me a drink of water from a barrel. It tasted terrible and I spat it out. Mor squeezed my arm.

"Johna," she said, "you must be still. This is all there is. Don't waste it by spitting it out!"

I didn't want Mor mad at me and leaned in close to her. I didn't understand why the water was so bad or why I couldn't have any food, much less why Mor would be angry at me for wanting these things.

In a little while even more Jews entered the loft. It was becoming crowded, with little room to move about without stepping on someone.

"How long are we staying here?" Mor asked Far.

"The moon is too full for us to leave tonight," he answered. "Any boats on the water would be visible. We will have to wait until tomorrow night to leave."

With a sigh, Mor stood up and untied a long rope that hung from a rafter. She tied it first to my waist and then to hers.

"Why are you doing that? I don't want a rope on me," I protested.

"I want to be sure you won't be pushed away from me in

this crowd or maybe fall off the loft. And I don't want to hear any more fussing from you," Mor said angrily, and the rope stayed on.

"I have to pee," I complained.

"I will take her for you, Margit," Emma offered.

"No, you just stay away from her!" Mor hissed back at her. I wondered why Mor did not like Emma. She turned back to me. "Oy, we have to go down the ladder and do it in the gutters." We climbed over people, back down the ladder, and found the cement potty behind a black tarp hung to give a little privacy. Mor still kept the rope on both of us.

"Hurry up, Johna...just squat down and go pee," Mor urged. She stood in front of me so no one could see. I tried to pee as fast as I could because the corner smelled so bad and I could see a man who was vomiting coming toward us. When I finished, Mor quickly pulled up my pants and we crawled back up the ladder to the loft. Once again we had to pick our way through all the people and some were not so nice about our passing through.

"I hate it here, Mor! Can't we go back home now?" I cried. I wanted food, and I wanted my own bed, my friends, our life the way it used to be.

No!" Mor snapped, but then she put her arms around me and hummed to me again. I loved it when she sang to me and I soon grew quiet.

The night seemed to stretch on forever. With all praying or groaning, and the soft whispers of those around us, sleep did not come easily, plus I itched all over. I could still hear the mice crawling under the hay and my head was filled with thoughts of the spiders and bugs that I knew had to be just about to crawl on me. Finally, unable to stand it, I climbed onto Mor's lap. The hours passed, and finally daylight began to slowly creep through the cracks in the barn walls. When it was light, the barn door opened and the farmer and his wife brought us warm milk and slices of bread. After going so long without food, the milk and bread tasted good. When we finished eating, twin girls about my age crawled over to me and we played a button game, using buttons from their mother's sewing kit, trying to see how many buttons we could match. We talked in whispers. It was fun, but all three of us had itching scalps and that constantly interrupted us.

When the early evening sun started to make the sky red, the barn door opened without warning and Erik appeared.

"Do not be afraid," he called up to us. "I have brought a doctor friend to help. We will be moving out tonight."

Erik climbed up to the loft and I saw he had on a black band just like the one Far wore. A man in a black suit followed him up the ladder. He wore a white armband with a red diamond in the middle and carried a doctor's satchel. A stethoscope dangled from his neck.

Far got up and joined Erik, then the two of them followed the doctor as he moved about the loft, stopping at each of the babies and small children. To some, he gave shots with a long needle. With others, he placed a white mask over their noses. I watched as he went from child to child, moving closer to me.

The doctor and Erik took Mor to the side and I heard the doctor ask, "What about this little girl? We must keep the children quiet. A shot, a precaution, a mild sedative, it will make her sleep."

Mor looked at Erik for a moment without saying anything. Erik nodded back at her and she turned to the doctor and nodded her head once. The doctor then came over to where I sat.

"What is your name?" he asked.

"Johna."

"That's a nice name!" he said. "Johna, I'm going to give you some medicine."

"I don't want a needle shot!" I cried out.

"Perhaps we will do something else to make you sleep."

"I don't want whiskey to sleep," I said and looked at Mor and Far for help.

In one quick move, the doctor pushed me down and sat on me, putting one of the white masks on my nose. It was filled with dripping, foul smelling liquid on the inside. The odor made me gag, and my face felt as if I were back in the ambulance being pressed into a pillow again. Everything turned pink and all I could hear was the loud beating of my own heart.

I don't think I was unconscious for long, and when I woke up, my heart raced with fright.

I couldn't see, nothing made any sense. I looked up at

the rafters of the barn loft and saw dark, terrible things moving there. I was afraid, but couldn't cry out. I tried to move my arms to fight the demons flying about above me, but they would not work right. Panic seized me, but then I realized Far was holding me and I calmed down. He gave me a drink of water. I had a terrible thirst after that awful nap and this time I drank it down gratefully. I looked around and saw the doctor was still there, watching me.

"I see she has awakened from the ether sooner than I expected. How about a shot this time to keep her quiet?" he asked Far.

"No! No!" I shouted. "Please, Far!" I pleaded. But he stayed quiet. I turned to Mor. "No, Mor! No!...Mor, I don't want a shot with a needle!"

Mor looked at Far and shook her head. Far turned me so that I was facing him.

"You're not a baby, Johna," he said, "but Far's big brave girl, right?"

"Ja, Far," I whispered, trying to keep from crying.

"Can you be quiet, Johna? Can you?"

"Ja, I can, Far. I was quiet in the ambulance, and hiding in the chest, wasn't I?"

He looked at me long and hard, searching my face.

"All right," he said at last. "But if you make any sounds or start talking tonight, I'll give you the shot myself." Far showed his fists to me, and I shook my head 'no' many times. Far looked over at the doctor. "We'll try without it. If she can't do it, I'll come get you."

The doctor shrugged his shoulders and moved off.

Not long after that Far had us all climb down from the loft. When everyone was on the floor, he did a head count, deciding how many would leave. Then he divided us up into groups. Bubbe, Zayde, Emma, Mor and I, and nine others were in one group. We would be the first one that would leave the barn.

The fifteen of us who were leaving first gathered together near the door. Mor tightened the rope between us and reminded me again not to talk. At a signal from Far, we moved out into the night. A heavy, wet fog blanketed the night and there was little light. We walked a long way in the dark, moving along a narrow trail through the rolling fog and wet grasses that slapped against our legs.

Gradually I became aware of a roar in the distance—it was a sound I remembered from the beaches we went to each summer, the sound of the sea. We climbed up over a little hump and then I could hear each wave as it surged up onto the shore. Far put his hand up to stop us. At his gesture, we all knelt down in the sand and waited for him to tell us what to do next.

Chapter 19

Exodus

Still connected to Mor by the rope, I sat shivering in the sand next to her. Far had disappeared into the fog down the beach. After a bit he came back to where we were all gathered.

"Follow me," he commanded, waving his arm.

We all got up and followed him over the beach toward the sound of the surf. I couldn't see well in the dark and stumbled over a beach log, hurting my foot.

"Ow! Ohhhh!" I whimpered. Mor picked me up and whispered, "Shh, be quiet or Far will give you a needle shot."

That was enough to stop my complaining.

We walked on until we came to a broken up cement wall. Far told us to sit there. A strong wind blew in from the ocean, pelting my face with loose sand. Mor wiped the sand from my cold face and tried to comfort me.

Far seemed to be waiting for something, but I didn't know what. He kept his eyes on the water, occasionally looking up and down the beach. After what seemed a long time to me, he stood up and peered into the night. Then he turned toward the rest of us and once again beckoned for us to follow him. People picked up their belongings and got ready to move.

Some, like the old man in the forest, had bundles of things tied in string. Some had suitcases, like we did. Still others just had pillowcases filled with things and tied in a knot at the ends. At Far's signal, we dusted the sand off from our clothes and walked to the edge of the sandy beach where the sea bubbled and foamed. Barely visible to me through the fog, a rowboat rolled with the waves.

Searchlights suddenly appeared and lit up the water between us and the small boat. In that light I could suddenly see Erik stood at the water's edge just before us. He was dressed in his shiny black boots and bulky winter jacket. He looked at me and smiled, then stepped over and picked me up in his arms. He waded through the ice-cold water toward the rowboat I'd seen.

Others followed, grasping outstretched hands until we were all hauled into the rowboat.

When Erik reached the boat with me, he whispered, "I'm not coming with you, my sweet Johna." He kissed me, his face wet and smelling of salt and seaweed. Then he lifted me up into the boat. He hugged Mor and helped her into the boat beside me.

Erik and Far both continued to help everyone into the rowboat until it could hold no more. Then Far jumped in and pushed off with an oar. I looked at Far's wet pant legs, then back to the sandy shore where Erik had already disappeared into the gray fog. I reached for Mor and held on tight to her.

The boat rocked as Far rowed away from the shore. The further we went from the shore, the higher the waves grew, pitching us up and down. Some sloshed over the sides of the boat and splashed seawater onto our faces and into the bottom of the boat. Suddenly the rowboat began to swirl in circles. Using the oars, Far struggled to stop the boat from spinning. Terrified, I hung on to Mor even tighter. The others in the boat held on to one another and the sides.

At last, with a loud clunk we bumped into the side of a fishing boat that hovered over us.

A long rope ladder dropped down from the fishing boat to our little boat. I stared at it—it was covered with slimy green moss and slapped against the hull of the boat as it bobbed on the swells. One by one, people began to climb it up to the bigger boat.

When it was my turn, Far untied the rope that held me to Mor. I stepped up on the first rung, grabbed the slippery ladder with my right hand and hooked the elbow of my short arm inside the rope 'rung' and held on. I was afraid to move, afraid I would not be able to hold on and climb at the same time without falling into the cold sea.

"Come on, Johna, you can do it," Far softly urged me.

The ladder twisted and turned with each movement of the waves. My hand slid when I tried to raise myself and I lost my grip, leaving only my left elbow holding me to the ladder as my body slammed into the boat. I screamed.

"Shush," Far said as he caught my legs in his firm grip,

leaving me hanging upside down over the water. My glasses fell off my face and into the ocean. Carefully, balancing himself between the bobbing rowboat and the fishing boat, he turned me right-side up again.

"Hold on to my neck, Johna," he whispered, and I hung on as tight as I could as he climbed the rope ladder, nearly choking him and leaving him gasping for air. Finally he lowered me onto the deck of the fishing boat. Then he climbed back down to help others. I stood alone on the deck of that strange boat, stomping my feet to get warm.

Emma, wrapped in a warm shawl with her face hidden behind a dark purple scarf, came over to comfort me, but remembering Mor's dislike of her, I pushed her away.

I sat down on the deck and pulled my knees up tight to my chest, looking through the forest of legs that grew as more people climbed into the fishing boat. Soon it was so crowded it was impossible to move, but I couldn't see Mor anywhere.

"Where is Mor?" I cried out in panic, sitting alone, afraid to move on the pitching deck. I want my Mor!" I hollered, but the other people just looked at me, their faces hidden in shadow. Finally, Mor found me and sat down beside me. She still had the rope she had used in the barn and quickly retied us together. She cuddled me close to her to keep us both warm. Emma moved over and stood right beside us—most of the other people remained standing on the deck. When there wasn't room for any more, the engine of the fishing boat roared to life and we began to move, quickly gaining speed.

Suddenly, the sound of a loudspeaker came from out of the fog, cutting through the noise of the engine.

"Halten Sie!" a man's voice cried. Then he shouted, "STOP!" but the fishing boat kept moving, not even slowing for a second. A blast of machine gun fire erupted out of the fog from almost straight out in front of where Mor and I were. Two people standing near us slumped down onto the deck and I saw dark spots of blood spread on their clothes. People screamed. I clung to Mor and screamed with all the others.

Three men helped the injured into the wooden toolbox at the bow of the boat. Everyone else scrambled down across the deck floor, falling over each other. Another burst of gunfire shattered the night and Emma tumbled down on top of Mor and me. I looked up as Mor pushed her off of us. I saw her try to rise up, then collapse.

Mor put her hand over my mouth and eyes, turned my head away from Emma and kissed me all over my face. Far pushed his way through the crowd toward us. He knelt down and gathered both of us into his arms. Then he saw Emma where she lay beside us, her chest red with blood, her eyes open.

"Oh, shit, Emma is shot. Alfred is going to kill me when he finds out...if we get out of here alive," he said, peering out into the dark.

"Who is Emma, Poul? What does she mean to you? Who is Alfred?" Mor sobbed. That scared me so that I began to cry, too.

"Margit, not now for questions. The German's are patrolling. They're firing at the sound of our boat. They may hear us, but they can't see us. The captain says we can get away through the fog. He is going to change course towards Malmo. Just hold on a little longer, Margit...I promise you, we'll be fine."

"Oh, my God! Are we all going to die, Poul?" Mor wailed. "I'm only twenty-seven and you twenty-nine. We're too young to die...and Johna!"

She had barely finished speaking when a man on the other side of the boat jumped over the railing and into the ocean.

"Oh, my God," she cried. "Now suicide!" She began to sob again.

"Shh, Margit! He didn't want to take the risk of being caught, but we can't help him now," Far said.

I pulled on Far's sleeve, "Are we going to be shot? Are we bad?" But Far didn't have time to answer. People began to push all the women and children, Mor and I included, toward some steps leading into a hatch below deck. We climbed down, hanging on as the boat hit wave after wave on the sea.

The hatch cabin stank with the odor of fish. Piles of nets and tackle and dried-out seaweed lay about the hold and added to the smell. In one corner a small lantern flickered, outlining oblong boxes filled with all kinds of fish. A small kitchen and two bunk beds were built into the walls. Benches and little tables had been shoved against the walls to make room for some of us to sit, but the rest simply sat down on the slimy floor. As we moved out farther into the ocean, the boat started to really pitch and roll, making most of us seasick. Many of us puked onto the floor.

"Mor, where are we going?" I asked. "Are we going to vacation with Thor in Sweden?"

Mor didn't answer me, but shoved me into a cubbyhole onto a mattress where another small girl lay sleeping. My hair had an awful itch, but exhausted, I fell asleep. I awoke to hear everyone on the boat shouting and screaming. Terrified, I looked around for Mor, but couldn't see her right away in the dark. I began to cry, but just then the hatch above opened, letting in both light and air. Far looked in and grinned down on us.

"We have landed! We made it...come up and see!" he yelled down.

We made our way back up the ladder to the deck where Far hoisted me up on his shoulders. Most of the people were crying and hugging each other. It was still dark out, but I could see the boat was tied up to a large dock where men in green helmets, dark tweed uniforms, and rifles slung over their shoulders stood all along pier.

"Who are the soldiers?" Mor asked Far. "Are we to be imprisoned here in Sweden after all? I see barbed wire to the left at a gate entrance. Are we still in danger? Are you sure Sweden was a safe place to go?"

"I don't know what to expect, Margit," said Far, "but I expect it's better than being shot."

People gathered around and prepared to go ashore. When it was our turn to leave the fishing boat, Far carried me down the gangplank and Mor followed us onto the pier.

"Stay put right here," he said, setting me down. "I will go help your parents." He walked back up the gangplank. He and another man made a chair with their arms and carried Zayde down to us. Bubbe followed slowly behind them.

Once everyone was on the dock, the soldiers separated the men into one line and the women and children into another. I watched Zayde limp over to the line of men, with Far still helping him. People screamed and hollered.

"We want to stay with our families," they yelled.

"You must do as we ask," said a soldier, calming them with his hands. "We are trying to help you. There is a reason for everything, and soon you will be back with your families."

Mor held onto my hand, and Bubbe stayed close to Mor. Soon we were escorted into an area fenced off with barbed wire. Inside the fence was a long building with steps leading up into it. It was an empty barracks. Inside, stacked against the walls in the corners, were old mattresses. Mor finally untied the rope between us. Then she moved one of the mattresses from the pile closest to us and set it on the floor so the three of us could sit down.

Other children broke away from their parents to race around the bare room. I jumped up and joined them. It was the first time we were free to run in many, many days. We were all thirsty and found a faucet where we crowded and shoved our way to the sink to drink. Some of the children saw my missing hand and backed away from me, staring at my short arm.

Mor was halfway across the room, coming after me and shaking her fist. "Johna," she called out to me, "we are not safe yet, and you must stay with me and be quiet or I'll tie the rope to us again. Do you hear me?"

"Ja, Mor," I said. "I just want to get some water!" She waited for me to get my drink and then took me back to the mattress she had pulled out.

The front door to the barracks opened and several women in white uniforms with red crosses on their hats entered, pushing a cart before them. Soldiers carrying rifles followed behind the nurses and took up stations beside the door.

"We will be passing out bottles of milk for the babies, and hot chocolate, doughnuts, and crackers for everyone else," said one of the nurses, pointing to the cart they had brought. When I heard that, in spite of Mor's warning, I jumped up and joined the other children as they ran toward the cart for food.

"Go back to your mothers! Now!" a soldier ordered. He and the other soldiers used their rifles to block us from the cart. It scared me so much I ran back to Mor and sat as still as I could on the mattress.

The nurses began to move the cart through the room,

stopping before each person to give them their rations. When the cart stopped by our mattress, the nurse said, "What are your names?"

Mor told her and she wrote our names and a number on three pieces of cardboard, which she then tied round our necks with twine.

"What is going to happen to us?" Mor asked the nurse. "No one is telling us anything."

"We have to process you in the manner of Swedish laws," the nurse said.

"When will we be reunited with the men?"

"We have to interrogate them first. Some will not be allowed to enter Sweden. They might be spies," the nurse answered.

"We're just Jews," said Mor in anger, "not spies! How can you treat us this way? Have we not been through enough?"

"I can't answer all your questions," said the nurse. She handed us the hot drink and doughnuts and then turned her attention to the people on the next mattress.

After I drank my hot chocolate and finished a doughnut, I folded up my blue money coat and put it down for a pillow to rest on, but my scalp itched so terribly I couldn't rest. Mor saw me clawing at it to make it stop.

"Oy! Johna is getting a red sore in her head from the fleas and lice. The bugs are taking over all of us. It is so creepy," she said to Bubbe.

"I have bugs in my hair, Mor? I'm afraid of bugs. I have bugs in my hair? I have bugs in my hair? Are the bugs making me itch? Make them go away! I hate bugs," I said, upset and frightened. The thought that it was bugs crawling around on my head only made it itch much more.

A soldier approached and called out, "Christensen!" Mor raised her hand.

"You and your little girl follow me," the soldier said, looking at the tags around our neck to check our identity.

"Please, could my mother come with us?" Mor asked him.

"No, just you and your daughter may go with me. She has another number and can't go with you. Let's go!"

The soldier with the gun scared me, and I closed my eyes

so not to see him. We followed him outside, across a dirt field to a building with a red cross that was just like the ones on the nurses' hats painted on the door.

"Do they hide Jews in here?" I said, opening my eyes just a bit.

"Johna, keep quiet!" Mor said, and pulled me close to her.

We walked down a hall that smelled like medicine, and the soldier told us to wait for a nurse. Soon, a nurse came toward us, and to our delight, Far was right behind her. Mor ran to meet him and hugged him, pulling me with her. He patted me on the head and whispered to Mor as she squeezed my hand.

"Ow!" I yelped, and she loosened her grip.

The nurse seated us on some stairs to wait our turn to get our picture taken. When it was our turn, they had us lean against a wall. Then I heard a click and saw a flash that made me see silver dots.

After the photos, Far, Mor, and I were led into a room with white walls and a white tile floor. In the corner stood two white bathtubs with chrome legs. A large clock hung on the door.

"I have to delouse you," the nurse announced in a matter-of-fact way. "We will start with a haircut and shampoo." She proceeded to cut Mor's hair and then mine, but Far's hair was already short enough. Next she covered my head in green gunk and soon my head tingled. Then it began to hurt, burning me.

"Ouch! Ouch! Rinse it off, it hurts!" I cried, but Mor held onto me, forcing me to sit still until they had rinsed the green gunk out of my hair.

"We must now use disinfectant salve on you and have you soak in the hot bath water for a while," the nurse said, and ran water into the tubs.

"I don't like you ordering us around," Far told the nurse. "It's degrading. There is nothing unsanitary about me or my family."

"Mr. Christensen, I have many people to process, and I'm very tired. If you won't abide by our rules, we will send you back to Denmark."

"You're very rude, and I want to know some answers!" Far demanded.

"Mr. Christensen, I will send in another nurse, if available, that might put up with you, but for now, take off your clothes, put your things in this bag, and I will find some clean clothes for you to wear," she snapped, and handed him the bag.

"Don't get mad at her, Poul, I don't feel safe yet," Mor said to Far. He only grumbled in response. As we undressed, he took my blue coat from me, and when the nurse wasn't watching, hid it under the bathtub. The nurse rubbed thick green salve all over our bodies, except for our faces. The gooey stuff made our skin a light green. It smelled like strong medicine and made me cough and sneeze.

"There is a button to push if you need a nurse sooner, but a timer has been set for you to soak one hour. Ring for a nurse when it goes off." She left, locking the door behind her. Far helped Mor and me into one tub, then he climbed into the other one.

"Are my parents being processed, too? Where are they now? I've got to know they're safe," said Mor, her words coming out all at once.

"I will find out," Far reassured her. "I'll have us all together soon."

"How will you do that?"

"I got you here, didn't I? We'll all be safe now, Margit. You can relax."

"Did they interrogate you?" Mor asked.

"They just asked stupid questions. I'm not a Jew or a refugee, and they couldn't refuse me entering their country."

"Mor, I have to pee," I whined. "My arm hurts when I pull it out of the warm tub water." Mor looked down at me and then gasped. "Look at Johna's arms, Poul, they're all red, like a sunburn. Push the black button to summon a nurse!"

"Ja! Damn, my skin is burning, too," Far said, and rang the bell for a nurse. A different nurse arrived. She was very tall with blond curly hair, and had a friendly smile. I could see she wore a red necklace under her white uniform.

"My name is Svea," she said, "and I will try to make your transition as comfortable as possible. Why did you ring? Your time isn't up."

"She's got to go potty," Far said, and pointed at me.

Svea pulled out a potty out from the cabinet. As she gently lifted me out of the tub, I felt a stinging sensation all over my body.

"OW! OW! OW! IT'S BURNING!" I shrieked, and began to bawl. It hurt so bad, I jumped up and down, flailed my arms, and then peed all over the floor. Blood was seeping from my skin onto Svea's white uniform as she held me.

"Do something!" shouted Far, jumping out of the tub. "What is wrong with her!? Call a doctor!"

"Oh, God, help her! Where is a doctor?" Mor screamed.

Svea quickly dusted me with a white powder and I watched my red body turn blotchy white. Soon the bleeding stopped and the pain lessened, though it still hurt. Then Svea dusted the white powder all over Mor and Far.

"The salve is too strong for Johna's tender skin and she should have soaked for only ten minutes, not forty-five," Svea explained. "Who was the nurse?"

"We don't know," said Mor.

Svea just shook her head and handed us some clothes. Mor put on a gray cotton dress, white socks, and brown tie-shoes. A too-large white sweater hung on her shoulders like a blanket. In my pile were some pajamas, along with black socks and slippers. Far looked funny in a pair of overalls and a dark green shirt. He had been given a pair of wooden shoes. We all looked at one another, wondering who these people in these strange clothes were.

Svea and Mor immediately seemed to like one another and Svea took us under her wing. She led us up to the nurses' station, where she made us some hot tea. While we drank it, she went into the bathroom to change her blood-stained uniform. She came back to us when she had finished.

"Margit...that's your name, right?" Svea asked, looking at Mor's neck tag. "You have had so much trouble within your country and I'd like to help your family. After you are through processing, I want you to come and live with my sister, my father, and me. We have a large house. We own a small grocery, and Poul can work for us until your family can get on your feet. Does that sound good to you?"

Mor hardly knew what to say, and finally, just managed to say, "Ja."

"Good!" said Svea, smiling at all three of us. "I will come for you at the refugee camp."

Across the room, Far smiled and held onto my blue money coat. Mor smiled at Svea, and held out her hand to her. Svea held it for a moment, then turned to me.

"Your short locks are cute, Johna. I like the way it curls around your beautiful face."

"Your red glass beads are pretty," I said, feeling I needed to repay her compliment. When I did, Svea unclasped the necklace from around her own neck and re-fastened it around mine.

"It's yours for being so brave," she said, and for the first time in days, I smiled.

Shortly after that, we were led outside to stand in a line again. Far found Zayde and Bubbe and brought them into the line beside us. Bubbe and Mor hugged one another tight.

"We didn't know if they were going to let us be with you," said Bubbe in a trembling voice.

Pretty soon some busses pulled up and we were ushered on board. Two soldiers with guns sat in the front seat.

"We are taking you to a refugee camp near here," said one of them. "They have rooms all prepared for you."

"Do you think Svea will come for us?" Mor asked. She moved close to Far and held his hand.

"I hope so, if not, I will look up Thor's family to help us. But I'll tell you, Margit, I can't live this way. I'm going back to Denmark. I will meet up with Erik, Thor, Arne, and my brother Orla to see how I can help them smuggle more Jews out of Copenhagen. I will also enlist in the Danish Brigade they have formed here in Sweden."

"Oh, Poul, please don't leave us," Mor begged.

"Margit, do not interfere with what I must do for Denmark. I promise to return as soon as I can, and I will wait to go until you and Johna and your parents are safe and settled, hopefully at Svea's or with Thor's wife. I need to make some money before I leave."

Mor said nothing more after that.

Behind us, Bubbe and Zayde sat praying and rocking in their seats as the bus rolled down the road.

Chapter 20

Endings and Beginnings

Our bus approached a wire fence and stopped in front of a large gate. We all got out of the bus and waited until shotgun-armed soldiers unlocked the gate. When they had opened it, we walked through and across the dusty gravel in front of yellow barracks. As soon as the last person had entered, the soldiers closed the gates behind us.

"The soldiers locked the gates, what are they doing?" said Mor, grabbing at Far's arm.

"Perhaps they do this to keep us safe and orderly. I really don't know," Far answered her.

A Red Cross lady came out to meet us and gave us the number of our barracks and room.

"Oh, please, can my parents have the room next to us?" Mor asked her.

"Certainly," said the lady from the Red Cross, "your rooms will be numbers fifteen and sixteen," and assigned Zayde and Bubbe the room next to us.

As soon as everyone had been given barracks and rooms, the Red Cross lady escorted us to what was to be our temporary home. Zayde, with Far's help, limped on his sprained ankle into their room first. We moved on to our room.

I peered in. It was small, and had one light bulb hanging from the ceiling. Along the wall of our room were two small beds with pillows, sheets, and folded blankets sitting on top of them. A wooden cabinet stood against the opposite wall. Next to it was a round coal stove with a note on it that read, " Boil Water Only." Also on that wall, there was a square sink without a faucet, with a bar of soap and two towels laid out on it. A nurse followed us into our room.

"At five o'clock we will ring a bell and you are to go outside to the roped off area to get instructions on the camp rules," she said, and then left us.

Far looked inside the cupboard and found some pots

and pans with notes on them that said, "For boiling water only." We all stood in the doorway and just looked at this tiny, bare place.

"At least the room is clean," said Mor.

Far ushered us into the room, but he did not sit down.

"I'm going to talk to the authorities that run this place. Don't worry, I will be back by five, Margit." Far kissed us both and went out the door.

Mor and I sat down on one of the beds and looked around the room again.

"Where's the toilet?" I asked.

"Outside, but you are not to go alone, do you hear me?'

"Ja, Mor...but Mor, what is an outside toilet? Can we go see?"

"No, we will see it later," said Mor.

"But, Mor, I have to pee!"

"All you want is to pee, pee, pee! Oj!" Mor said, and to my surprise, she laughed. She took my hand and we walked down the long hall to the front entrance. As we passed the other rooms, I peeked through open doors and saw other people just sitting on their beds and saying nothing.

"How long do we have to live here, Mor? I miss Hanne."

"Ask Far later."

"Mor, my skin still hurts...and my eyes are watery without my glasses," I said, but Mor did not say anything more.

Outside, we came to a small shed. Mor opened the door. Inside I saw a bench with a hole in it and a terrible smell hit me that came from inside the shed.

"That's your toilet," Mor said. She pulled my pants down and lifted me up to sit over the hole. "Hurry up, Johna."

"I don't have to pee now," I said. The smell had scared my need away. Mor shook her head and put me down. After she used the toilet, we went back to our room.

Far was not back yet when the bell rang for us to go outside and hear the rules, so we went without him. We stopped to get Zayde and Bubbe, but neither of them wanted to leave their room.

Outside, a soldier stood on a platform inside the roped-off area. When we were all assembled, he began to speak.

"Welcome to our camp," he said. "These are the rules of

the camp. There is a faucet at the entrance gate for you to fill your buckets with water. The coal bins are out in the front of your barracks. The building on your left with the large 'H' over the door is a hospital for your medical needs. You may receive Care packages and tobacco in the hall of the hospital. We will be serving meals twice a day in the dining hall. You can line up now for dinner, as it will be served soon."

After the soldier left, we stood in line taking in the smell of food that drifted through the door of the dining kitchen. One by one, we filed by the cooks, who gave us chicken soup and bread.

"Please, may I take some soup and bread to my parents?" Mor asked a server. "They are not well and stayed in their room," The server told Mor that would be fine and gave her a tin container for soup and bread, but Mor had to sign a paper to take it out of the dining room. After we finished our soup and bread, we took the tin to Zayde and Bubbe's room. They were both asleep, but I woke them with little kisses.

"Thank you for being so thoughtful," said Zayde, taking the soup from Mor. "Where is Poul?"

"I don't know, but I'm sure he will be here soon, Papa," said Mor.

I sat on Zayde's lap while he ate, and he stopped now and then to give me bites of his bread. Bubbe and Zayde were still tired and didn't talk much, so after a while, Mor and I returned to our room. At long last, Far came in the door. Mor explained the rules of the camp to him and asked him what he had found out.

"I chatted with the director and shared a meal of meat and potatoes with him. It is a good thing that you brought my birth certificate because he gave me a release paper to come and go from the camp, since I'm not a Jew. Their Swedish King Gustav is sympathetic to the flight and the problems of the Jews," said Far. "The director gave me some money coupons to help us buy personal needs."

"Poul, Johna is complaining that her skin is hurting and it is all red and scaly," said Mor, showing Far my arms.

"No, it doesn't look good," said Far. "I'll take her right now to the hospital building and have them look at her. Come on, Johna, let's go."

Far took me to the building with the big "H" on the front. In quick order, a doctor there came and looked at my rash and gave me some ointment. Then he gave me an eye test. When he finished he said I would get a new pair of glasses.

As the days passed at this new camp, I found other children to play with. We ran around the compound playing Germans and Danes in hide and seek, and in games where we pretended to be shooting each other. We found sticks that became our pretend rifles and hit each other with them until the grownups caught us at it and put a stop to the game. We also made circles and wrote our names inside them with small rocks. Sometimes we drew a big Danish flag in the dirt with sticks to mark its boundaries. I thought of Hanne often and wondered what she was doing, and if she were afraid living with Germans.

One day we received word that my new eyeglasses had come. To my dismay, they were heavy, ugly, brown ones, and far too big for me. I had to squint and wrinkle my nose to hold them on my face, so Mor tied them on with string. This was uncomfortable, but it was just one more thing that felt strange in a sea of them.

Far was gone a lot during these days, coming and going from the camp to the town. He only ate with us sometimes, as he didn't like the kosher food the camp prepared, and only occasionally did he spend the night with us. I don't know what all he did, but one day when he came back he talked of trying to find Thor's wife.

"I can't seem to locate Thor's wife. Maybe she moved," Far told Mor.

When I heard Thor's name, I remembered what he had said that day in Uncle Orla's pawn shop about having a doll for me in his hotel room, and a great hope sprang up in me.

"Remember the Swedish doll Mr. Pehrrson had for me, Far? Do you have it for me?"

"No, Johna, forget about the doll," said Far, but it was not so easy for me to do. I had lost my Jette somewhere on our journey, just as I had lost Erik, and Hanne, and my doll house before that.

I wasn't the only one who mourned, though. Whenever

I visited Zayde and Bubbe in their room, they were always sad. Zayde would talk, but it was almost more to himself than to me.

"I don't have my beloved violin to play," he'd say. "Where are the rest of my family and children? What has happened, and where could they be? What is their fate? Where is God?" he would whisper over and over again.

"Zayde, is God a grownup?" I asked him one time, trying to understand where God might be if he weren't with us.

"Johna, go to your mother!" he shouted at me. "You speak like your father!"

I knew he did not want to play with me anymore, so Bubbe took me back to our room where she stayed to visit a little with Mor.

Several days after that, however, something nice happened. Svea came to see us, and brought along her father, Mr. Sjoberg.

"With Poul's help, we finally have permission to remove you from this camp. Now, we will be responsible for your family's well being!", she said, pointing to her father and herself, as she smiled at us. "I want you to know, too, Margit, that my father and I are also working to find a Jewish family where your parents can stay, but that has not been easy."

Mor and I hugged and thanked them both for their wonderful help.

A week later we moved in with Svea in the town of Ystad. We had our own room, and Mor and Far helped Svea's father in his grocery store. Svea did not have a husband, so she spent a lot of time with me.

One of the first things we did together was she began teaching me to speak Swedish, and in a short while I started attending a Swedish School. During Christmas I was even in a Christmas pageant. I wore a white dress with a green wreath around my hair. I followed behind a girl who was playing the part of Santa Lucia, the saint who brings light to the winter season by walking about wearing a wreath full of burning candles on her head. This was the happiest time I had had since the last time Hanne and I had played with our napkins.

Life at Svea's was fun for me in other ways, too. Down

the road from her house was a big barn with horses painted on the side where her friends had a riding stable. Large trees with long strings of moss hanging from the branches grew beside it. In the spring, the grassy green fields where the horses grazed lit up with little bright yellow flowers. Svea gave me riding lessons at the stable, and Far was proud of me for being such a tomboy.

It took several months, but Svea finally found a place for Zayde and Bubbe to live. It was a small room in a Jewish family's home, about three miles from us. Far had stayed with Mor and I all this time, and now Zayde and Bubbe were nearby. It seemed as if life were finally better for all of us.

Then, one evening as I was lying still in my bed in the room that Mor, Far, and I shared, I heard Far talking to Mor.

"Margit, yesterday I volunteered with the Swedish police battalion for the Danish Brigade Army. I will start training tomorrow morning and must leave tonight," he told her.

"You gave me no warning you were doing this, Poul!" Mor cried out. "Please! After all we've been through...please don't leave us!" She clutched at him.

"I told you already that I was going to help Denmark. A man has to do what he has to do," Far told her. "You and Johna are safe now, so now's the time for me to go."

"It's dangerous, Poul, you could get shot," said Mor, and began to cry.

"Stop it! I will send you money and come and visit you when I can. I told you I have to do this."

I sat up in my bed, looking at them. "Far, are you going away?" I asked in a soft voice.

Far looked over at me, and then came and lifted me up in his arms, holding me tight.

"I'm going to Denmark, Little Skat. You take care of Mor."

"The Germans are in Denmark. Don't go there," I said, but I knew Far always did what he said he would.

Mor and I could only stare at him while he packed his clothes.

"Tell Svea and her family good-bye for me," said Far. Mor and I kissed and hugged him, smearing him with our tears. Then he went out the door.

It was two months before Far sailed again from Denmark to visit us, and he was gone again two days after that.

Our life continued on at Svea's. I went to school and Mor helped Svea's father in the store. Then one Saturday a few months later, Mor let me spend the night with Zayde and Bubbe. Far was sailing from Denmark to visit us in Sweden again and he wanted to be alone with Mor.

I was glad to be with my Zayde and Bubbe again. I always missed seeing them. Zayde was still quiet and sad, though, and I wanted the old Zayde back again.

"Zayde, I wish you could play me a song on the violin," I said, thinking of the fun times we had had when we all lived in Denmark.

"The violin has no more music to play. It is broken, Johna, like my heart. I will read you a good story from the Bible instead." Zayde sat down with me and read me a story about Jonah and the whale. When he finished, he said to my surprise, "Let's go for a nice walk with Bubbe and go visit Far."

Bubbe and I both stared at him.

"Why would you want to do that?" Bubbe asked.

"He is an impossible man," said Zayde. "But I talked to God, and I must make amends and try to like Poul. He was very brave, helping us, and I have a need to tell him this."

"All right," said Bubbe, and went to put on her things.

We had strolled a few blocks on our way to visit Far, when suddenly Zayde fell down before us on the sidewalk.

"Zayde! Zayde! Are you shot? Get up," I whimpered over him, but he did not move. Bubbe knelt down beside him, but then she began to cry, and pulled me away from him.

"He is in God's hands, now, Johna," she said, holding me close to her. "He is in God's hands."

In just a short time, an ambulance came and took him away.

At Zayde's funeral, Mor's brother, Uncle Willy, sat next to us with his wife, Marie. Mor hummed a song in my ear to keep me from feeling sad.

"Shush, Malka!" said Aunt Marie. "How can you have such bad manners, to hum at your dear father's burial? You must have surely learned that from being married to Poul. Have you no shame?" Marie scolded, just as they lowered Zayde into the grave.

Mor could only look at her in surprised silence. Far was furious, and took us away from the graveyard as soon as Zayde had been buried.

One day I said to Svea, "Would you like to see my little hand? Does it look like an elephant foot to you? Is it ugly?"

"Sweet Johna, don't keep saying that to me. It is cute and you can do everything that people with two hands can do," she said, kissing my little hand. "Now, Johna, we must go to town today and buy some more school supplies for you."

It was almost spring, and the wind blew the new leaves from the trees, shuffling and sorting them around the fields while Mor, Far, Svea, and I walked down the road to the People's Store in the downtown of Ystad. Families of ducks and geese followed by little ducklings and goslings crossed the road, and we walked around them to let them pass. I smiled as I watched the cute babies waddle behind their parents.

"Let's take this shortcut through the woods," Svea said. We moved off the road and into the thick woods. Above us, the wind rustled the branches of the trees. The day had been cloudy, but the sun broke through and lit the path through the forest in scattered patches of light and dark. I reached up to take Svea's hand.

"What's wrong, Johna?" Svea asked.

"I'm afraid," I whispered back.

"There's nothing to be afraid of," she said, and squeezed my hand tight.

But I kept silent until we came out of those woods.

"Svea, can I talk now? Will the Germans hear me?"

"Oh, dear Johna! There are no Germans here to hurt you. They can't harm you here in Sweden," she said, and drew me close to her side.

In town, we walked along the sidewalk past the different stores. I lagged behind Far, Mor, and Svea, looking into the windows at all the different things on display. I stopped suddenly in front of one them.

"Johna, get over here with us," Mor called back to me.

"Far, Far! Come and look!" I said, motioning toward the window. They backtracked to where I still stood.

"Remember your promise?" I said jumping up and down in excitement and pointed at what I had seen in the store window.

Mor and Far looked in the window and exchanged glances. As Far reached into his pocket and started to count out coins, I saw tears come to his eyes. He went into the store while Mor and I stood looking in the windowpane, holding hands. When he came out, he was holding something behind his back.

"Little Skat, cover your eyes!" said Far. When I had them covered, he said, "Now open them!" And there before me was my own red umbrella.

Epilogue

I wish to thank the readers for letting me share this story of my family's escape from Denmark when the Nazis began to round up the Jews in that country, and the sudden events that led up to it. It has been written as I remembered it.

I thought it had been our own story, but I learned later in life that the Danish people worked together to save over 7,500 Jews that night we crossed the cold, dark sea to Sweden, ferrying them across in hundreds of small boats like the one we were on—each one loaded to capacity with tired, frightened people taking with them only what they could carry.

I had many frightening memories of that time. Images would burn in my mind and fill me with unease. I tried to talk to my parents about it, share my experience and learn about theirs. However, neither of them would ever talk about the war years. I don't know if it was because they thought it was better for me not to know any more than I did, or if it was because it was too painful for them. Mor was never again the happy person she had been before the war. I knew for myself some of Far's experiences. Remembering, in particular, the night he cried under the stairwell after seeing three of his friends killed in the park by Nazis.

Nevertheless, these memories were in my mind and soul for nearly sixty years. I tried to just go on, live life as if these things had not happened, to deal with it alone. I tried to shut down my feelings, telling myself, "I was too young and cannot remember." But I did remember. And so, I started to write about it, to confirm and validate the memories with other family members.

Each image, every event, was still so vivid to me. As I began to write, I was once again a six-year old, trying to make sense of that which is senseless, and that is how I told the story—from that six-year-old's eyes.

Our story went on after leaving Denmark, of course. My mother, my Jewish grandparents, and I, were in exile in Sweden for eighteen months. It was a long time for me to miss my extended family and my Danish friends. Far came and went, living almost a separate life from us, but never abandoning us. He had said he would take care of us, and he always did.

After Zayde passed away, sweet Bubbe was lonesome without him and she grieved deeply. She was legally blind, so my mother and I would visit her often and clean her room where she lived. I would sit on her lap and look out the window with her, but I doubt that we were seeing anything remotely similar. She still let me comb her long hair, and she still always had candy for me, but everyone seemed to have changed; we were not so happy as we had been after the escape.

While we were in Sweden, one of my father's sisters, Aunt Eva, lived in our apartment after we abandoned it. She wrote to us of the problems they had with the Germans. She sold all of our belongings, and many other possessions just disappeared. Our dishes, clothes, my toys, my napkin collection, and even the cedar chest in which I had hidden in were all lost.

When the war ended we sailed back to Copenhagen on May 29, 1945. Bubbe, Mor, and I arrived in our homeland along with 2,500 other refugees. Far was still there. When the ship docked we stood on the deck looking at all the Danes screaming joyously, welcoming us home and waving Danish flags. It was an amazing moment, but we did not see any Jews on the dock.

Some were still hidden in Denmark, some had perished in the concentration camps, and some had simply disappeared.

My father stood in the welcome crowd. He looked handsome in his Army uniform. He waved to us, and then, to my surprise, he held up my beloved doll, Jette, for me to see. I thought I had lost her somewhere in those awful days before we arrived in Sweden, but he had found and kept her safe for me. My father also brought a mink stole for my mother, two minks with their noses connected. It wasn't her old mink coat, but she was pleased with it.

As for coats, I never again saw my blue coat that Zayde had made for me, and have no idea what happened to it. I don't even know whether my parents lost the money that had been sewn into it, or that which Far had put behind the molding in our apartment. The money my father had placed in a Swiss bank for safe keeping was never recovered.

Erik—brave, handsome, and kind Erik—and Far's Swedish friend, Thor, both died mysteriously during the war. I don't know what happened to my father's German friends Alfred, Carl, or Myra, for no mention was ever made of them again.

In 1948, Far decided we should move to America. When my mother told Bubbe that we were going to move to America and that we couldn't take her, Bubbe was heartbroken. She was also angry with my father for abandoning her, and for taking Mor and I away from her. It was little solace for her that according to her own tradition, my mother's responsibility as a wife was to be with her husband. Mor tried to reassure her that we would often return to Copenhagen to visit her, but Bubbe could not forgive the move.

My father sailed for the United States first, leaving us to wait in Denmark until he found work and a place for us to live. My Danish Uncle Taus lived in America in Snohomish, Washington, and was our sponsor. When we applied for immigration, the American National Immigration Service refused entry to my mother because she had a handicapped child. It took us six months to prove that I had a birth defect and not a handicap. Proof included letters from schools and a doctor, and I had to show that I could dress myself, tie my shoelaces, even that I could knit and sew.

Eventually our application was approved and we sailed on a huge ship named *The Bactory*. I still remember my first sight of the Statue of Liberty in New York.

We stayed first with some distant Jewish relatives. Then we moved to Snohomish. After we had been there long enough to get on our feet, we moved to a new home in Solana Beach, California, where my father had found carpentry work.

My father's ambition had been to be an architect. He had taught himself to draw and design floor plans, with the help of his friend Thor. He never achieved that but he did design and build a house for us in California, complete with a swimming pool and gas rock sauna. Because so much money had been spent for our home, however, my father decided we couldn't afford to visit our relatives in Denmark. And so we never saw Bubbe again. In 1952, four years after we came to America, she fell and broke her hip.

She died soon after that and was buried in the Jewish cemetery in Copenhagen.

In 1953, I was sixteen and without the waiting for a stork as I had as a young child, I found myself with a younger brother, David, and later a sister, Linda. I was pleased to have younger siblings, but by the time Linda was born, I already had a family of my own and was living in Idaho.

In 1963 my mother was diagnosed with Scleroderma. In spite of trips to Tijuana, Mexico, for experimental shots and specialized treatment, she died on December 11, 1964. She was only forty-eight years old. My father informed me that during her last hours she spoke only Yiddish. I was nine months pregnant with my second child at the time, and could not travel to her funeral.

My father sent me her necklace, a Star of David, which I wore ever after. Even years after her death I found myself wanting to call out to her as I did during those times when she was hiding in the hospital during the war.

On October 15, 1965, my father was trying to light the sauna by the pool, when the leaking gas exploded, killing him. The death of both my parents within a year of each other left me with an emotional void and an ache deep inside of me, but I gained in other ways by getting to know my brother and sister when they came to live with me.

The small copper chest that my father's best friend Erik had stolen from the King's Palace now resides in the Danish room of the Nordic Museum in Seattle, Washington.

My Jewish Grandparent's menorah candelabra and two wine goblets, and my mother's mink stole, remained in my family, along with two small dainty swastika handkerchiefs that my father had gotten from the German lady, Myra. Sadly, my red umbrella is long gone.

In 1999 I went to Israel and walked in the Holy Land where my Zayde had so wanted to live. I visited the Wailing Wall and felt as if he were with me. The Wall itself was like a magnet, binding together my Jewish heritage and all the survivors of the Holocaust. I wrote a note with the names of my deceased Jewish family and friends on it, and like thousands of pilgrims before me, I placed it in the crack in the wall. Zayde would have said the names ascended to heaven. I also visited the Yad Vashem Museum and saw the small forest where one tree had been planted in my name for having been a survivor. I took in the Resistance and Rescue exhibition honoring the Danes and others that saved so many of us in those perilous times.

In October of 2000, I returned to Copenhagen, Denmark, carrying both my parents' ashes. Standing on the shore and looking across to Sweden, my Danish family and I spread my father's ashes onto the waters of Orsund Sound. Part of my mother's ashes resides with her mother and with the rest of our Jewish relatives in Moishe Cemetery. The rest of my mother's ashes were put to rest in the King's Garden under a beautiful oak tree, across from where she grew up.

For me it was a deep, emotional accomplishment, and brought a certain closure to have them at rest in their native soil.

I hadn't seen my relatives in Denmark since 1976, but I had cause for celebration when the Methodist Church sponsored a free trip to Israel, including two days in Copenhagen in 1999.

Especially soul stirring for me was meeting up with Svea, the Red Cross nurse who had so generously taken us all into her home. She was 91 years old.

We had corresponded all those intervening years, and when we met again, Svea asked me to sit on her lap again, just as I had done in Sweden in 1943, when I was that little girl. We both cried. I felt much love for her.

I also took time to revisit the Danish synagogue where Mor and I used to go with Zayde and Bubbe. It also aroused my soul. I looked down from that familiar balcony and the innermost feeling in my mind and heart was that of being a Jew. My family agrees that I have my mother's heart and my father's spirit for adventure. Somehow their differences reconciled in me.

For many years I participated in the Washington State Holocaust Education Resource center in Seattle as a member of their speaker's bureau. I also belonged to the child holocaust survivor group in the Seattle area. As a result of these associations, in 1986 I had the honor of presenting the Raoul Wallenberg Medal of the America Jewish Heritage Society to the Danish Vice-consul at

Washington State Capitol in Olympia, who accepted it on behalf of Queen Margaret of Denmark.

I'm proud of my father's deeds and his heroism in saving us and many other Jews. Stories like mine must be told and not forgotten. Future generations must know and not forget us.

Safe Side of the Sea

Winds flow to me as I descend the hill to the beach below Fort Casey.

Across the strong current of Admiralty Inlet sits the low silhouette of Fort

Flagler on Marrow Stone Island, and Fort Warden stands to the west of

The historic buildings of Port Townsend.

I haul lumpy books and paper to write overdue answers to letters

That demand more than my good intentions. The books remain unread—

My blank paper remains unblemished as I rest in the afternoon sun.

Behind, in the concrete bunker eight-inch guns remind me

Fort Casey once formed one corner of the "Triangle of Death."

My thoughts wander to World War II, reminding me to never forget my

Plight as a six-year old Jewish girl in Denmark, facing persecution and

Having to make a dangerous exodus across the Kattigat and the North

Sea to neutral Sweden.

On the beach of freedom I say a prayer for the family I lost and I

Watch the never-ending rhythms of the seashore.

Flapping herons hear me across the sand;

Seagulls call and fly free like kites in the wind.

All the unidentified birds whose names I do not know cast a spell on me.

I lie here empty, open.

I have no choice but to remember that dangerous past and be thankful

I am on the safe side of the sea.

- Johna Christensen

Acknowledgements

There were numerous friends, relatives in Denmark and professionals that helped Johna with her ideas and writing along the way. Among those were members of the Whidbey Island Writers Group, Sharon Nicholson, Dorothy Read, Roy Gray and Vincent Mark Hagel. Vincent spent many hours with Johna helping write a different version of this story called "Hidden in Plain View". It became clear that Johna's personal story, told in her own voice as a child, would be more powerful, and she rewrote everything. However, Vince's help in getting something going was important. I would also like to thank Sarah Stamey and Robin Ireland of Bellingham, Washington for editing Johna's writing prior to this publication.

After Johna's passing, her family tried to continue her pursuit of getting a publisher through a traditional submission process of publisher rejections. Fortunately, the self-publishing industry has changed significantly recently. So, I would also like to thank Chuck and Dee Robinson, owners of Village Books in Bellingham, Washington for being one the first in the country to have an in-store self publication process. This finally made it affordable to get this done in a prompt fashion. Rod Burton, Graphic Designer, provided graphics and advice for putting it all together.

Lastly, I would like to thank Johna's family and organizations, like the Holocaust Education Center, for keeping the history alive and to...never forget.

- David Earl Christensen

Biography

(The following was written by Johna Christensen prior to her passing)

I was born in Copenhagen, Denmark on July 26, 1937. The illegitimate daughter of Jette Malka (Margit) Pressmann (Mor, or Mother, in Danish). My mother had used a drug during her pregnancy, to minimize symptoms of morning sickness, but they did not know that birth defects were a side effect, and I was born with a deformed arm & hand. Mor's parents, Orthodox Jews, had fled Russia during the pograms of 1906 and settled in Copenhagen. My grandparent's names were Brochr Miriam and Yechiel Jacob Pressmann. My grandfather was a Tailor by trade. Because my father, Poul Villy Christensen, was not a Jew, the Pressmann family could not accept my parents' relationship. In spite of this, my parents were married anyway, when I was two years old. My grandparents were in their seventies in 1943 and lived near the Synagogue in a retirement complex.

My mother (Mor), Jette was 27 and my father (Far) was 29 in 1943 when we were forced to make our escape to Sweden. My father was a carpenter in Copenhagen, and was an atheist, which made relations with my Jewish grandparents difficult. My Danish grandmother, Poula Christensen, who also cared nothing for religion, was a proprietor of the Café Absolon in Copenhagen. Many Germans congregated there for the good food, drink and company of the parlor girls. Since the two families had little in common, there was a great deal of tension as my father engineered our escape.

After remaining in exile in Sweden for two years, the war ended. On Tuesday, May 29, 1945 we arrived back in the Danish harbor along with 2500 other Danish refugees returning to our homeland. My father was still enlisted in the Danish Brigade Army, but was yearning to return to his trade as a carpenter and restore a better life for our family. All our valued possessions were gone, and when my father tried to reclaim the money and jewelry that had been left in Swiss banks for safekeeping, it could not be found.

My Jewish Grandfather (Zaydeh in Yiddish), Yechiel, died and was buried in Sweden before the end of the war. My grandmother (Bubbe in Yiddish), Brochr died in Denmark in 1952.

Late in 1948 my father, mother and I immigrated to America. My parents had two more children after arriving in the United States. In 1964 at the age of forty-eight, my mother (Mor) died of scleroderma, a rare systemic autoimmune disease which hardens the body's vital organs. She had always longed to visit her native Denmark, but never did after arriving in America. She spoke only Yiddish in her final hours.

Ten months after my mother's passing, at the age of fifty-one, my father was fatally injured in a gas explosion at a home-made sauna in his custom home in Southern California. He had sought the American dream, but never really attained it. To me, he was an adventurer and a brave Viking hero.

I was twenty-eight years old when my parents left me the challenge of raising my little brother David, age 11, and my smaller sister Linda, age 7, along with my own three children. They are all responsible adults now with their own families.

I am now a sixtyfive year old grandmother, living on beautiful Whidbey Island in Puget Sound in Washington State. I still correspond with the Swedish Red Cross ladies, Ebba and Svea, who are in their eighties.

These days I actively participate in a speakers' bureau, where I have received a humanitarian award for keeping alive and sharing my memories of the Holocaust. I have been a guest speaker for the Anti-Defamation League, surviving Generations in Seattle, and the Danish American Cultural conference. I have also spoken at Dana College in Nebraska, Portland State University, the Northwest Cultural Conference in Oregon, the Holocaust Centre Society in Vancouver, and other organizations. In addition, I am especially well received by students in public schools.

I would very much like to see my story shared with others in the hope that it will stimulate a greater sense of caring in our times.

As part of this publication you will find a newspaper clipping (with translation) dated May 29, 1945 showing our family's return to Denmark. A separate photo enlargement is also attached of me with my mother and father.

Johna, Poul (Far) and Jette (aka Mor, or Margit). May 29, 1945 photograph for cover of Land Og Folk *newspaper, upon return from Sweden.*

Johna (2nd from left) next to best friend, Hanne Hansen (3rd from left), and other neighborhood friends. Taken approximately 1943 in Copenhagen.

*Brochr (Bubbe), Johna and Yechiel
Pressmann (Zayde), 1939. (Johna
is 2 years old)*

*Johna holding new glasses, 1940.
(3-1/2 years old).*

*Poul (Far) in Carpenter work
clothes, 1941. (27 Years old)*

Poul (Far), 3rd from left with cigar, at construction site with fellow workers, 1941.

Poul (Far), in street clothes with friend. (Possibly Eric Hansen), 1942, 28 years old.

Pressmann (Jewish) family. Yechiel (Zayde) is 6th from left, with Johna (3 yrs. old) on lap, next to Brochr (Bubbe) with thick eye glasses. 1940.

Yechiel (Zayde) with Brochr (Bubbe).

Christensen (Danish) family. Jette (Mor) is standing with white blouse 2nd from left. Poul (Far) is 7th from left sitting on floor with necktie. Poulene (Farmor) is sitting in center of portrait, 9th from left. Daughter, Ruth, is in white dress on her left, next to Olaf (Farfar).

Svea (Swedish Red Cross) and Johna in Sweden with temporary eye glasses, 1944.

Johna on Svea's lap, May, 12, 1999 with a first reunion after 55 years.

Det blev en overstrømmende Modtagelse i Frihavnen i Gaar, da de første hundrede danske Flygtninge kom hjem med den svenske Færge „Malmø". Paa Billederne ser man Flygtninge paa Færgen inden til deres Slægtninge i Land, og et Medlem af Den danske Brigade, der maatte tage i Forvejen, men som nu var nede at hente sin Kone og Datter. Gensynet var hjerteligt.

15 danske Statsborgere for allieret Krigsret

Aarhus, Mandag (RB)

Efter Ordre fra den allierede Overkommandos Efterretningstjeneste er følgende internerede i Aarhus sendt til København, hvor de skal for en allieret Krigsret, alle sigtede for Spionage.

Direktør Oscar Wanschneider, Aarhus, Direktør Erik Barnow, Marselis Boulevard 18, Aarhus, Købmand Kai Gothenborg, Rileskov, Vintherborg-Petersen, Hornsnæsvej 17, Lage Kaster Boising, Aabybøj, Antikvarboghandler John Gustavsen, Valdem 12, Aarhus, Søren Peter Kjær, Niels Juelsgade, Aarhus, H. Fanggaard, Mørkegade, Aarhus, Ivar Mathiesen, Rileskov, Svend Aage Nielsen, Langelandsgade, Aarhus, Svend Nikolaisen, Frijsendal, Hamsel, Selmer Rasmussen, Aarhus, Svend Stengaard, Aarhus, Olav Strøm, Klostergade, Aarhus, M. R. Villadsen, Aarhus.

Man ved, at flere af de sigtede har været Medlem af tysk Sikkerhedstjeneste. De 15 blev paa Rejsen til København bevogtet af den danske Brigades Feltpoliti.

Krigsforbryderne for Retten om faa Uger

London, Mandag (RB)

Reuters Bureau meddeler fra det øverste allierede Hovedkvarter: Den øverste amerikanske Raadgiver for Krigsforbryderkommissionen, Dommer R. H. Jackson, udtalte i et Pressemøde i Dag, at Retssagerne mod Krigsforbryderne antagelig kunde begynde om faa Uger.

Der var to Kategorier af Sager:

1. Sager angaaende Forbrydelser mod Medlemmer af de amerikanske væbnede Styrker, hvorved Krigens Love er blevet overtraadt. Disse Sager forberedes af Generalstabsadvokaten. 2. Naziforbrydelser mod Indbyggere i de nazibesatte Byer. Disse Sager vil blive henvist til de stedlige Domstole.

Det ledende Princip vilde blive at spore Forbrydelserne til Roden og ikke standse ved ubetydelige Underordnede, der udførte Forbrydelserne, men føre Slaget direkte mod Magtens Stede, hvorfra Forbrydelserne blev ledet. Krigsforbryderne vilde blive dømt for Handlinger, som i ethvert Land og endog i deres eget i mere oplyste Tider, havde været betragtet som Forbrydelser i Aarhundreder.

FØRSTE 2500 DANSKE KOM I GAAR HJEM FRA SVERIGE

De fik en overstrømmende Velkomst baade i Frihavnen og paa Hovedbanegaarden

I Gaar kom ca. 2500 Danskere hjem fra Sverige, dels med Færgen fra Malmø og dels fra Helsingborg, og det blev en straalende Velkomst dem til Del. Den første Færge gik fra Malmø Kl. 8 i Gaar Morgen, og tidligt fra Formiddagen var der tæt med Mennesker ude i Frihavnen, Familie og Venner med Blomster og Flag spændt ventede paa, hvornaar Færgen vilde vise sig. For at være sikker paa at komme i rette Tid havde en stor Del af de Ventende...

mange maaske store Skilte, hvor man f. Eks. kunde læse „Velkommen hjem! Tulle, Walther og Irene!"

Kl. ca. 11 gled Færgen ind i Løjet, men Hurraraabene var begyndt længe forinden og stilnede først af, da Færgen var helt inde, og gjaldt det om at finde hinanden. Det lykkedes meget hurtigt, for begge Parter — baade dem paa Skibet og dem i Land — var jo lige ivrige, det lød med Hilsener over Rælingen, og man baade lo og græd.

Tale af Minister Mogens Fog

Saa talte Minister Mogens Fog — fra en Højtalerbil ved Landgangen: ...

Finlands Overgang til Freden forløber lettere end ventet

Udtalelse af den socialdemokratiske Redaktør Virtanen

Stockholm, Mandag.

(RB's særlige Korrespondent)...

Luftmarskal Tedder kom i Gaar

Den britiske Luft-Marskal Sir Arthur Tedder kom i Gaar Kl. 13 til Kastrup sammen med Lady Tedder, hvor de blev modtaget af General Dewing, General Gørts, Viceadmiral Vedel, Forsvarsminister Ole Bjørn Kraft og flere andre. Fra Lufthavnen kørte Selskabet til Palace Hotel, hvor General Dewing havde indbudt til privat Frokost. I Eftermiddag modtog Kongen og Dronningen Sir og Lady Tedder ledsaget af General Dewing, i Aftes var Regeringens Værst ved en Middag.

Dansk Landbrugs-Delegation til England

For at forhandle om Priserne paa danske Landbrugsprodukter

General Dewing med Stab modtages paa Raadhuset

Billedet viser Lady Tedder, Luftmarskal Tedder og General Dewing ved Modtagelsen i Kastrup Lufthavn.

Universitetet udnævner 8 Æresdoktorer

Programmet for Københavns Universitets Frihedsfest den 4. Juni er nu fastlagt. Der indledes med en Kantate, og derefter taler Rektor magnifikus, Professor, D. theol. Jens Nørregaard...

Nødvendige Varer og Raastoffer fra Sovjetunionen

STADIGVÆK DAARLIGE FORHOLD FOR DE RUSSISKE KRIGSFANGER

Nu maa Myndighederne snart tage sig sammen

Store Fremskridt er der ikke sket i Forholdene, siden de russiske Krigsfanger blev flyttet fra KB-Hallen til Jægersgris. Her er i Øjeblikket indkvarteret 450 Russere i Alderen fra 1 til 75 Aar. Der ventes yderligere godt 1000 russiske Krigsfanger i de nærmeste Dage. Og det bliver af trygtelige Slid for de mange, der frivilligt har paataget sig det vanskelige Arbejde at hjælpe Russerne heroppe.

Tyskerne bortførte alt Inventar

Da Lejren blev overtaget efter Tyskerne, var alt, Senge, Sengetøj, Tæpper, Porcelæn...

Offentlig Indsats nødvendig

Fortsættes Side 3

Newspaper English Translation

LAND OG FOLK (Land and People)

Copenhagen, Tuesday May 29, 1945

(Photo inset): It was an over flow reception greeting in Freeport yesterday, when the first 2500 hundred Danish Refugees came home on the Swedish ferryboat " Malmø." In the pictures you see Refugees on the ferry waving to the Danish Kinship of their land. Also pictured is a member (Poul) of The Danish Brigade, who took on their emotions of it all, but now was down to fetch his wife (Jette) and daughter (Johna). The reunion here is heartwarming.

(Article below Homecoming photo): FIRST 2500 DANES CAME HOME YESTERDAY FROM SWEDEN
They got an overwhelming welcome in both Frihavnen (Freeport harbor) and at Hovedbanegaarden (Central train station).

Yesterday 2500 Danes came home on a ferry from Malmø, Sweden, and some from Helsingborg, and it was an overwhelming welcome. The first ferry from "Malmø" arrived at 8 in the morning. Many people were out at the harbor already, family, friends with flowers in arms and Danish flags anticipating and waiting. There were also many cardboard posters which read welcome. One large poster said "Welcome home! Tulle Walther and Irene!"

It was approaching 11 am, and the happy ferry landing had begun way before it arrived, but somehow it had a tranquil atmosphere with many anticipating finding each other on land or on the boat. The lucky ones will spot their families right away and they were eager to greet them all, looking for them at the boat railing and also with tears.

(Other Headlines from this Front page):
Danish Agricultural Delegation to England.
To negotiate the prices of Danish Agricultural

Finland's Transition to Peace
Precursor easier than expected.

Opinion of the Social Democratic Rdaktor Virtanen

15 Danish nationals for the Allied court-martial

War criminal Rene to the Court in a few weeks

Air Marshal Tedder came yesterday

STILL DEPRESSED RELATIONSHIPS
FOR THE RUSSIAN PRISONERS OF WAR
Now the authorities must soon get its act together

University Appoints 8 honorary Doctorates

Poul (Far), Johna, Jette (Mor) portrait in November 1945

Poul (Far), Johna, Jette (Mor) portrait in November 1945.

Photo of poles where Johna witnessed Danish Resistance Freedom Fighters shot by Nazi's on Østerbro Street, 1943.

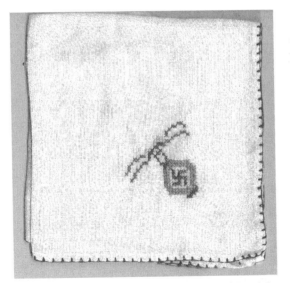

The Swastika handkerchief, Johna observed.

The copper chests allegedly stolen by Erik Olsen from the King's Castle.

Farmor waving to Johna from her apartment above the Absalon Café, from a visit in 1976. (The Café at Aslongade 21 is no longer there)

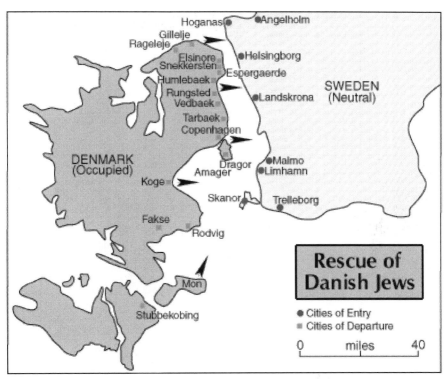

Map of the Rescue of the Danish Jews to Sweden.

Small rescue boats bringing Jews to the fishing boats in the Harbor

One of the many types of fishing boats bringing rescued Jews to Sweden.

Danish refugees register in Sweden after escaping from Nazi's in Denmark.

Johna at computer in 2001, teaching school kids about her experiences in WWII.

Johna visiting Israel in 1999, at the dedication honoring the entire Danish nation as "Righteous Among the Nations," in recognition of the campaign to save Denmark's Jews in the autumn of 1943.

For Further Viewing and Reading
Bibliography:

Videos:

A Day in October (2006), Tango Entertainment, Starring D.B. Sweeney, Kelly Wolf, Format: DVD

Flame and Citron (2010) Nimbus Rights II APS, Starring Thure Lindhardt, Mads Mikkelsen, Directed by Ole Christian Madsen. Format: DVD

Miracle at Midnight (1998) Davis Entertainment, Disney Educational Productions, Walt Disney Television, Starring Sam Waterston, Mia Farrow, Directed by Ken Cameron Format: DVD

The Danish Solution (2003) Narrated by Garrison Keillor, Directed and Produced by Karen Cantor & Camilla Kjaerulff. Format: DVD

The Power of Conscience: The Danish Resistance and the Rescue of the Jews (2007), Direct Cinema Limited, Starring Danish Anti-Nazi Resistance fighters Directed by Alexandra Moltke Isles. Format: DVD

Books:

Ackerman, Peter and Jack DuVall. *A Force More Powerful* New York: Palgrave, 2000.

Benchley, Nathaniel. *Bright Candles: A Novel of the Danish Resistance*, Harpercollins Childrens Books; 1974

Burgan, Michael. *Refusing to Crumble: The Danish Resistance in World War II (Taking a Stand)*, Compass Point Books, 2010 .

Byers, Ann. *Rescuing the Danish Jews: A Heroic Story from the Holocaust*, Berkeley Heights, NJ, Enslow Publishers, 2011.

Clemson, Barry. *Denmark Rising*, Cybernetica Press, Inc. , 2009.

Goldberger, Leo. *Rescue of the Danish Jews: Moral Courage Under Stress*, NYU Press, 1988.

Hæstrup, Jørgen. *Secret Alliance: A Study of the Danish Resistance Movement 1940-45, Vol. 3*, Odense University Studies in History and Social Sciences, Odense University Press, 1977.

Jespersen, Knud J. V. No *Small Achievement: Special Operations Executive and the Danish Resistance, 1940-1945* Odense, University Press of Southern Denmark. 2002.

Kieler, Jorgen. *Resistance Fighter*, Gefen Publishing House 2008.

Flender, Harold. *Rescue in Denmark*, Unites States Holocaust, 1980.

Lampe, David. *The Danish Resistance*, Ballantine Books; First edition, 1960.

Levine, Ellen. *Darkness Over Denmark: The Danish Resistance and the Rescue of the Jews*, Holiday House, 2000.

Loeffler, Martha. *Boats In the Night: Knud Dyby's Involvement in the Rescue of the Danish Jews and the Danish Resistance*, Lur Publications, 2004.

Lowry, Lois. *Number the Stars*, Sandpiper, Reissue ed., 2011.

Lundbak, Henrik. *Danish Unity: A Political Party between Fascism and Resistance 1936-1947*, Museum Tusculanum Press, An article from: Scandinavian Studies, 2003.

Mills, Sonja. *The Danish Play: A True Tale of Resistance*, Playwrights Canada Press, 2004.

Moore, Bob (editor). *Resistance in Western Europe* (esp. Chapter on Denmark by Hans Kirchoff), Oxford : Berg, 2000,

Pundik, Herbert. *In Denmark It Could Not Happen: The Flight of the Jews to Sweden in 1943*, Gefen Books; illustrated edition,1998.

Reilly, Robin. *Sixth Floor: The Danish Resistance Movement and the RAF Raid on Gestapo Headquarters* March 1, Cassell; illustrated ed., 2002.

Roussell, Aage. *The Museum of the Danish Resistance Movement 1940-1945: A short guide*, Copenhagen, Denmark, Nationalmuseet; 6th edition, 1968.

Schoenberger, Elsebeth. *Birgitte's War: A Novel of the Danish Resistance*, Cameron & Co, 2011

Sutherland, Christin. *Monica, Heroine of the Danish Resistance*, Canongate Press, 1991.

Thomas, John Oram. *The giant-killers: The story of the Danish resistance movement, 1940-1945*, Taplinger Pub. Co; First Edition ed.,1976.

Toksvig, Sandi. *Hitler's Canary*, Roaring Brook Press, 2007.

Tveskov, Peter H. *Conquered, Not Defeated: Growing Up in Denmark During the German Occupation of World War II*, Hellgate Press, 2003.

Werner, Emmy E. *A Conspiracy Of Decency: The Rescue Of The Danish Jews During World War II*, Basic Books, 2002

Werstein, Irving. *That Denmark Might Live; the Saga of the Danish Resistance in World War II*, Macrae Smith, 1967.

Yahill, Leni. *The Rescue of Danish Jewry; Test of a Democracy*, Jewish Publication Society of America, 1969.

Cultural Institutions:

The Museum of Danish Resistance 1940-1945. The National Museum of Denmark, Frederiksholms Kanal 12, DK 1220 Copenhagen K.

THE DANISH RESISTANCE, United States Holocaust Memorial Museum 100 Raoul Wallenberg Place, SW Washington, DC 20024-2126

Nordic Heritage Museum, 3014 NW 67th Street, Seattle, WA 98117

Made in the USA
Columbia, SC
18 July 2023

20585323R00129